Growing Through It

Surviving Childhood Trauma, Abuse and Neglect

Ella Frick

TABLE OF CONTENTS

FOREWORD

Irrespective of cause, all pain has one thing in common, the redemptive potential to make an individual better. It is my hope that by sharing with you my experience, you will be branded with an acute sense of empathy for fellow humans attempting to navigate life the best that they can.

Being a survivor of compound childhood trauma, neglect, and every form of abuse imaginable, I have experienced the pitfalls that can come from unresolved trauma and I can attest to the damage it caused in my life. I can also attest to the power that can be found when a survivor is empowered and allowed to heal and use their experiences to grow and heal others.

As a business leader, entrepreneur, motivational speaker, mentor, podcaster, and author, I have had the privilege of guiding many women and men on their own journey of self-discovery, healing and growth. In this book, I will share my personal experience with trauma and growth. The walls are down, the mask has been removed and my vulnerability, pain, triumphs, successes, lessons, and failures are all found in the upcoming pages.

May my words bring you comfort, empowerment, inspiration,

and healing.

Chapter One

UNMASKING

I have lived so much of my life, hidden by shame, lacking an identity, fighting who I felt like I was and putting on a game face of "I'm ok". For 40 years, I have been the pretty girl. The girl who can light up a room like a football stadium on Friday night. I exuded light and happiness and hope, all while I was dying inside. The outside image of me was one that was expertly crafted. I was a chameleon and a people pleaser. I was a "great friend", because I always listened and was there to support everyone else. I knew that if I were listening, no one was paying attention to what I might have to say about myself. I would sacrifice whatever I needed to, to prevent me from revealing too much of who I was. I was your "closest friend," but upon deeper inspection, you never really knew much about me. You might be asking yourself, what did I have to hide? How bad could it be? My truth and my story may not be significant to you, but undealt with, it nearly ruined me. I am finally unmasking myself, in part to heal you, but ultimately, I know that this is my only hope to heal myself.

I had to learn who I was apart from my pain and trauma. When life begins under such extreme circumstances, you don't grow and develop in the same way that others do. I am not even sure I recognized myself as a person until I was an adult. I was so focused on the external world that I couldn't begin to learn about myself. Growing up in environments with instability, abuse, neglect, and impoverishment can create stress and trauma that look like classic PTSD, such as what soldiers experience after returning from war, and it affects development. Sadly, this condition of childhood PTSD had become so prevalent that clinicians created a specific term to classify it: Developmental Trauma Disorder. While this diagnosis was not a thing when I was growing up; I also grew up not seeing a doctor regularly, so it would not likely have been identified in me. I believe that there were adults outside of medical doctors who realized there was something very wrong in my life, but they may not have been equipped or empowered to intervene. Childhood trauma is classified as an event that a child finds overwhelmingly distressing or emotionally painful, often resulting in lasting mental and physical effects. Common causes include physical, emotional, and sexual abuse, grief, neglect, substance misuse, witnessing domestic violence, medical trauma, bullying, mental illness, separation from loved ones, as well as war and terrorism exposure. None of those things should be a part of our lives as adults let alone being part of our developmental structure as children.

One-time exposure can be enough to have a lasting impact on children. Repeated exposure to these events is called "Compound Trauma" which is classified as repetitive and prolonged trauma. For me, my childhood was a series of compound traumas, roughly twenty years of it. How, in a world that is so developed, with abundance surrounding us, can children experience a childhood that is akin to surviving a war zone? As a survivor of childhood abuse, it boggles my mind.

We need to be empowering our communities to protect our children. Author and professor, James Garbarino, who has a specialized study in what causes violence in children, how they cope, and how to rehabilitate them said "The initial trauma of a young child may go underground but it will return to haunt us". Notice his choice of words, he implies it will hurt the abused child, but he clearly states it will hurt us; us as a society. In researching the long-term effects of childhood trauma to better learn about myself, I learned that survivors struggle with having a sense of safety, they have an altered perception of reality; our brains are wired to expect danger, our flight, fight or freeze response is easily activated, we struggle with having close relationships, we have increased stress hormones flowing throughout our bodies, and we often have serious behavioral issues. Yes, yes, and yes- sadly, these are all true of me. So, I sought out to understand more about the why behind my feelings, behaviors, and actions.

A traumatized brain is "bottom heavy"; our prefrontal cortex which is our thinking center is underactivated when affected by trauma, which results in difficulties in concentrating and learning. The amygdala which is our fear center is overactivated which results in difficulty feeling safe, calming down and sleeping. Our anterior cingulate cortex which is our emotion regulation center is underactivated which impacts our ability to manage emotions.

Children are remarkable, we learn to survive unthinkable abuse by adjusting and accommodating to the abuse in ways that change our development. Knowing this about how the trauma I experienced impacted me on a physiological level , helped me to understand and unravel my story in a way that would serve me, my healing, and my future.

If you too are a survivor of childhood trauma or complex childhood trauma, it is my hope that the story you are about to read about my life and how I coped both healthily and unhealthily, and my growth and my perseverance through it all, will inspire you to heal, grow, and impact those around you.

If you are a "normal" person and you believe that God has put a child in your path, that you can help, please do. I pray that my story will guide you and inspire you. You may be the only hope that child has, to find a path to normal.

Chapter Two

THE FORMATIVE
YEARS OF ABUSE

I was born in 1980, to two young teens. My father was a charismatic guy, played football, loved cars and was a child abuse survivor. The latter descriptor is important in setting the stage of my story. I don't know all the gory details of the childhood he experienced, but what I have pieced together over the years shows a thoroughbred pedigree of victimization. He was beaten repeatedly by his stepfather, for no other reason than having been alive. I know very few stories from my dad's childhood, he just doesn't discuss it. The one story he tells in part, is the time he was beaten so severely he landed in the hospital, not expected to survive, and ended up losing his spleen. My grandmother, his mother, was not a woman who should have had children. She was mentally ill, the exact diagnosis is unclear, but I suspect she was a narcissist and potentially bipolar. Because her conditions were left untreated and unaddressed, she transferred her pain and suffering onto others.

I know very few details of my dad's relationship with his mother and have very few stories to go off of. A story that I can recall, is my dad saying that my grandma was like Imelda Marcos, she had hundreds of pairs of shoes, labeled, and categorized and she would have my dad and his brothers go and retrieve the shoes that matched her various outfits and then return them to their proper place. If you, like me, were not familiar with who Imelda Marcos was, she was the first lady of the Philippines before being driven from power, she was known for her lavish spending habits and huge shoe collection.

From what I gather, my grandmother was busy impressing people, and keeping her husband from killing or maiming her children, the best she could, which she was not successful at. While she was able to prevent extreme abuse from occurring with her other three children, she was unable to fully protect any of her children from the trauma.

My relationship and perception of my grandmother and her husband is an important narrative in my personal story. From what I understand and a bit of what I remember, I spent a lot of time with my grandmother and her second husband, the abusive stepfather. I was the first grandchild and completely adored by them. Now, I have fewer actual memories of this time, than I do stories to refer to. Some of the fonder memories I have involved swimming, apparently, I loved to swim, and they would take me out on boats and to pools and catered to my obsession with the water. I don't recall any of that except for one small memory of a sailboat. I also do not have any fond memories of holidays or birthdays or anything that I would deem as being "normal" memories of a granddaughter visiting her grandparents. There are a few distinct memories that I have of my grandmother, one early on, is my grandmother parading me around in a fashion show that she and her friends were putting on and she was commenting incessantly about my beauty and my blossoming body, another involved a modeling photo shoot which resulted in my photo being displayed in a store window for years, which she believed was all about her and her beauty. Exterior appearance was paramount in my grandmothers' life. We always had to look the part.

Another memory is from when I was about nine years old, my grandmother lived in a town in Northern California that overlooked a beautiful lake, Lake Konocti, and she had this grand house with white shag carpeting, detailed wooden furniture-to include credenzas (that was the first I had ever heard of this word, but it sounded as regal and as important as my grandmother prided herself on being), she had two miniature poodles, one white and one grey, and rooms full of clothing and shoes.

On this visit, my dad had driven me the hour or so, over a winding mountain roa, to drop me off to stay at my grand-mother's house. I think this detail stuck out to me because my dad did not ever take me anywhere outside of our annual trip each summer to see his biological father and half siblings in Southern California, where we would go to amusement parks. I am not sure how long my visit was intended to be, but I am thinking it was scheduled to be a month or more. Shortly after I arrived, which was about 11am, my grandma asked if I was hungry and I was, so she said she would make me a "Chef Salad", which sounded fancy and delicious, so I agreed. She prepared me the salad and when I sat down to eat it, I noticed that the little chunks of cheddar cheese were covered in blue and green spots of mold. I promptly mentioned it to my grandma, and she stunned me by replying that I was to eat it because she made it for me. I refused and she persisted, nearly forcing the rotten food down my throat as I cried, gagged, and sobbed. After eating the food, she forced me to eat, I vomited because it was rotten, and she punished me for disrespecting her. She grabbed me by the arm and dragged me into a bedroom, and said that I would stay there until I learned some respect. I remember thinking to myself that I hated her, hated my life and I just wished that my life could be normal. The next day, she came and let me out of the room, at this point it was nearly 24 hours since she locked me in the room and said that I could do chores to apologize for my disrespectful behavior the night before. While I wanted to argue and let her know that I should not be forced to eat rotten food, I stayed silent to avoid more trouble.

The chores she started me on was dusting all her furniture. While I dusted, she was standing over me and telling me about how much things cost and which man in her life had bought it for her. I have not yet told you that my grandmother was married a handful of times or more; marriage was a career business for her. I once answered when someone asked me what I was getting for Christmas, "a new grandpa" because that is what I got most years. These men would shower my grandmother with lavish gifts and in turn do the same for me to impress her.

After the dusting, my grandmother had me return shoes to the appropriately numbered and categorized shoe closet. My dad's stories were true, this woman had thousands of pairs of shoes. After the shoes were neatly put away, my grandmother hands me a brush and tells me to start brushing the carpet. The brush was a palm sized, heavy, wooden brush with short black bristles, like a brush that ethnic people might use to brush their hair. I had never heard of anyone brushing carpet before, so I stood there for a few moments and likely had a confused look on my face. My grandmother was getting annoyed, she quickly grabbed my arm and yanked me to the floor with her, and proceeded to show me how to brush the carpet in the proper direction. After demonstrating to me how to perform the chore properly, she said she was going out for a while and when she returned, I needed to have the entire house finished. The home was approximately 4,000sq feet with most of that being blanketed in the fluffy, white carpet. So, for hours and hours I was on my hands and knees brushing this carpet in "small stokes, always in a clockwise motion, moving around the room from left to right". You all, this was white, medium length shag carpeting- there was minimal impact my brushing was making. It looked just the same, even though I followed the directions explicitly, to include not walking on the freshly brushed carpet. After about six hours, my grandmother returned, arms full of shopping bags and she was in a bubbly mood, that is until she laid eyes on the carpet. She immediately started yelling at me, asking me why I was so lazy and why I couldn't listen. She ripped the brush out of my hand and started beating the tar out of me. Needless to say, the white carpet was no longer white.

I was so terrified and alone, I ran off, walking down the side of a highway, in an area I had never been to, not knowing where to go and not having an ability to call anyone for help.

My grandmother made no attempt to come after me. I'm not sure if that was reassuring or crushing; did she not care enough about me to make sure that I was safe. I continued to walk until my dad pulled up next to me in his beat-up toyota truck; he had driven over an hour to come get me, after my grandmother called to tell him that I was worthless and lazy.

To this day I cringe when I see a wooden hairbrush and we have never spoken of that day or event since. I never received an apology or an explanation. Silence after the abusive episodes would be the "norm", which taught me that "we" move on from trauma rather than processing it. Cope the best you can and move forward, never looking back was what I was being conditioned to do.

Years went by before I saw or heard from my grandmother again. I would hear about her from time-to-time; mainly I would hear from my great-grandparents or uncles that she was "up to something again". What they were referring to this time in particular, was her going back to college to pursue another degree. She had three or four degrees already by that time, and she was focusing heavily on learning Spanish.

My step-grandpa, the one that nearly killed my father and caused him to lose his spleen; his name was Walt, but I can refer to him by no other name than monster. Walt was a below-average looking man, with a large bald head and big face and a large white belly covered in wiry brown hair, that would protrude over his pants. He would wear blue, red and white striped suspenders each day over his stained white tee shirt, which would hold up his faded blue jeans. He followed creepy, child molester sterotypes and drove a rundown, blue van with a bed in the back. He lived in a single-wide trailer in a "family" trailer park and one of the two bedrooms of his trailer was set up as a perfect children's bedroom, even though he lived alone. If I were to identify a child abusing monster from sterotypes alone, he would tick every box. It would later surprise me to hear that he was even worse to others, than he was to me. I was not his only victim. I suspect he victimized every child he had access to, regardless of gender or relation.

I have no memories of him that do not include abuse. Not physical abuse, like my father suffered, that would have been preferred. No, he victimized me in the most shameful way a man can hurt a child. He stripped me of my dignity, my childhood, my innocence, and left a hole in my heart that would fester as an open wound for years to come. I was sexually abused by him from my earliest memories until I was in elementary school. I could say that I was eventually rescued from the abuse and that rescuing healed me, but that would be a lie.

I am not sure how things should have gone, but I suspect in a "normal" life, it would have gone much better than I experienced. You see, when I was about 6 years old, I had two police officers show up at my school to speak to me. They pulled me out of class and brought me into a room by myself- no parents, teachers, or other trusted adults with me and said, "your grandma called to tell us that she thinks your grandpa has been touching you inappropriately; has he?". I am not sure how that conversation ended or even what happened after hearing my darkest secret slip into the room like an unwanted guest. My innocence was spilled onto the floor, like a well of ink, and no one seemed to bat an eye. I was crushed and they continued talking. I know that I made it home from school that day, but I couldn't tell you how or when. Normally my mom would pick me up and drive us home to my great-grandparents' house, but I don't recall seeing my mom that day. My mom and dad never spoke of the allegations or the abuse, not then, and not ever. It was an ominous and silent wall that would further seperate me from them.

When I got home that night, my great-grandmother was giving me a bath and just before I stepped into the tub, I recall she said something like, "the police came to the house today; your grandma and Walt got into a fight and she called and told them bad things that were not true". I looked up at her and in barely a whisper I said, "but Noni, they were true", and she said, "you are a good girl Angela, and good girls do not speak of those things, you understand me?". "You will be ok honey, now get into your bath". And that was it. Maybe in her mind, that bath cleansed me of the abuse and we could all move on. What she didn't know and what I was too young and too afraid to express, is that the monster had been threatening me for years. He had forshadowed this truth from escaping into the bigger world. The sexual abuse was over after that day- well from him at least, but the mental anguish, fear and anxiety within my little mind and body began to grow.

I am sure it is not unusual for an abuser to threaten their victims, to keep them quiet, that is likely abuser 101,but my abuser was an over-the-top monster. He took me to the fair once and told me that he was able to get us special and private access to the grounds and rides, because his friends worked there. I loved the fair. This particular fair was called the Citrus Fair, the theme and displays were all citrus related and the air through- out the grounds smelled divine. There were large, magical cre- ations all made out of fruit. I would walk the fairgrounds in awe and splendor; amazed that people created such wonderous dis- plays from something so basic as fruit. It was something that I looked forward to each year.

The Ferris Wheel was my favorite ride and the thought of having it all to myself was so exciting. I remember getting on the ride that day and it taking off and I felt so special, on top of the world if you will, that I was so cared about, that I would get this special treat. We went around probably two full rotations before the Ferris Wheel car stopped at the top. I had never minded heights, and I used to pretend that I was living in the clouds when I was in high places. I would stop to dream and imagine this alternate world up there in the clouds. It took me only a few seconds to snap out of this dream world to realize that my abuser had not taken me on this "special" ride to treat me. Not only had he planned to assault me, he also had planned to terrify me. After sexually assaulting me, he proceeded to hang me from my legs, from the top of the Ferris wheel while threatening to drop me unless I promised to never tell on him for the "special love" we shared. At that moment, I was past being terrified. I was suspended eighty feet in the air, with only a monsters grip to keep me safe from falling to my death. The irony of this, even as a small child, was not lost on me; this monster was going to kill me either way. He would either release his grip and I would fall and perish, or he would pull me back inside his arms and I would be given the chance to die a slow and self-destructive death. As I began to plead, beg and promise, I surrendered to my powerlessness when I realized that the grown adult man standing at the operator's panel of the Ferris Wheel was laughing and cheering my abuser on. In that moment, I was taught that no adults were safe and that calling out for help was useless. I never looked at the fair the same again, but that was the least of the damage I would face in the years to come.

The threats were not delivered that dramatically going forward, there were plenty of threats, threats that included harming my family; or killing us all, including himself, if I ever told on him. After the police were involved, I did not see my monster again for many years. I am not sure if this was his choosing, or if my great-grandparents had stepped in to prevent him from having access to me. My dad had no relationship with Walt for those years, which may have also been a factor in the separation and distance.

My dad was an addict and when I was twelve-ish he started going to NA (Narcotics Anonymous) and AA (Alcoholics Anonymous) and "got clean". During this time, he met a woman and got married; shortly after she discovered she was pregnant. Coincidently, as part of my dad's recovery he decided to make amends with Walt. Now, I do not want to harshly judge anyone, and I have not had to battle addiction or recover from it. But from the outside looking in, I had to question how and why a person would make amends with someone who nearly killed them as a child and later repeatedly sexually assaulted and tortured their daughter, but that is what happened. So, the year my sister was born, I happened to be visiting my dad for Thanksgiving (this was not a regular occurrence) along with my younger brother who was maybe four at the time and Walt was attending Thanksgiving unbeknownst to me until he arrived. I had not seen him in about six years, and I was flooded with fear and anxiety. I believed in my head one of two things: that he came to poison all of us, to make good on his threats to me, or he came to molest my new baby sister. I had no allies at this dinner, there was not a responsible and trustworthy adult in attendance, at least not from my vantage point. So, I did what I felt any good big sister would do and I pulled my little four-year old brother aside, and I told him that someone poisoned the food and no matter what, he was not to eat even one bite or he would die.

Looking back now, through my adult lens I realize how terrifying that must have been for my brother. I either looked crazy or convincing, because neither he nor I ate a single bite of food that day. I think back to that day, sitting around this table of specially prepared holiday food, watching my "family" eat and enjoy themselves, while I sat there fully prepared that they were about to die. I was literally waiting for them to start keeling over, foaming at the mouth, slumping face down into their mashed potatoes and gravy, or whatever poisoned people did. I am not sure if I should laugh or cry at how absurd that childhood memory is. Most adults can look back with fondness surrounding memories of the holidays, but I struggle each year during those joyous times; in part because I don't have happy memories as a child, but also because I lived in fear each time my family would gather that the monster would be there to strike revenge in one fell swoop.

My family, they did not die that day, but a part of me did- that part of me that had been holding on to hope that my family loved me and wanted what was best for me, and that they would begin to protect me. I learned that Thanksgiving Day that all chances of those things being true were a fairytale.

If I were to be safe, the effort would need to come from me, and me alone.

I mentioned in the paragraph prior that my dad was an addict. Now, I want to be clear that given what I know about his childhood and how compound trauma impacts abuse survivors long-term, this makes sense to me. I don't hold a grudge or blame him for needing an out. He used drugs and alcohol to cope and survive. I have long ago come to terms that my dad was not equipped for a single day of his life to be a parent and that his choices and decisions were not about me. Now, does that make my shitty childhood any better to stomach- no. But viewed through this lens, I can apply empathy for what he endured and how he struggled and suffered through his own interactions with the monster.

As I mentioned, my parents were both young teens, who attended high school together in Oregon State, when I was conceived. I am not sure about the details of how they met and what drew them together, but by the time I was born, they were living with my dad's grandparents in Northern California. Their history and relationship is another undetailed mystery imbedded within my life story.

My relationship with my parents was unique. I think it would more closely resemble that of a sibling relationship, when there is a large age gap. We were parented alongside each other by my dad's grandparents. My great-grandparents, affectionately referred to as Noni and Papa, were just amazing people, hardworking caretakers of their daughter's poor relationship choices and offspring. Yes, these were the parents of my hairbrush yielding, psychotic grandmother. They had a very large three-story home, where my parents lived in a bedroom on the first floor close to the garage and I had a bedroom upstairs across from Noni and Papa. I rarely saw my parents. They spent most of their time in their room and likely were stoned during waking hours. During the years we lived in this house, my great-grandparents were my primary caretakers. I recall very little interaction with my mom or dad and the interactions I can recall were not full of tender, loving moments. I do have a faint, recurring memory of my mother singing me a song, "raindrops keep fallin on my head, they keep fallin". That song would pop into my head randomly for years, but it wasn't until recently that I looked up the actual song and read the lyrics. The song is about overcoming. Maybe this was the best comfort my mom could offer me. Maybe she believed that this night-time anthem sung softly to me on most nights, would give me the courage to wake up each day and fight the worlds battles with my tiny fists.

My childhood was gritty. My dad's biological father lived in Los Angeles and by my view and standards was leading a "normal" and productive life. We would go visit him most summers and I would get to visit the homes of celebrities (Tom Selleck, Shelley Long, Paul Mitchell) and to all these neat places (City-Walk, The Grotto and The Reagan Presidential Library to name a few) where he was working as a highly successful and sought-after landscape architect. On one of these trips, the first time I can recall us going to Disneyland, we had driven the nine hours from Northern California to Southern California and that entire trip I was riding in the trunk area of a hatchback car. While this was just as dangerous and sketchy as it sounds, in comparison, this was one of the better parenting choices my parents made.

I was so excited to go to Disney, I did not complain about riding in the cramped truck tucked in among our luggage; I toughed it out. To help you better understand how difficult and against my character riding in the trunk of a car was, and without a seatbelt, I want to share a story with you from when I was four years old. During a trip to Oregon to visit my mother's siblings, who were young adults, my aunt wanted to take me for a drive in her convertible beetle. In the early 80's in Oregon, seatbelts were optional and not a requirement, so this car didn't have any. I refused to go for a ride, citing how unsafe this would be. I was an odd kid, but I was principled when it came to safety. But on this trip, my desire to see Mickey Mouse far outweighed my desire to be safe.

Unfortunately, on that trip we only got as far as the parking lot of Disneyland, because my parents were busted for cocaine use while in our parked vehicle shortly after we arrived. They just needed a little bump to enjoy the happiest place on earth with their daughter. At this point in my young life, these types of situations were my norm, so I don't recall being upset or scared or embarrassed; likely I was not even disappointed.

My childhood was full of these colorful and disgraceful stories, of parties, drug raids, violence and poor examples of adult choices. Like the time my mom and her best friend cooked up this idea to get back at my dad when they were separating and they called the police and said my dad had a gun and was going to kill everyone where my mom worked, which happened to be a preschool. So, the police attacked my dad on site at the school to talk to my mom at her request, while I and a school full of children sat by and watched. Or all the fighting, the lack of stability, the lack of food, money, shelter, emotional support, etc. My dad loved my mom and chased after her. My mom was unable to love anyone it seemed or atleast she was blocked from expressing her love. So I watched this passionate and misguided man fail repeatedly at life and at his marriage. He was always failing at life and she was hardworking and miserable. They were a disastrous match.

I am not even sure what to say about my mother. She is a human version of the rubix cube. She has sun-kissed blonde hair with the perfect amount of wave to it, golden sun-tanned skin and smokey blue eyes. She was beautiful, but in a very Medusa kind of way. Her beauty would lure you in, but there was nothing good there for anyone. She attracted men to her. Men who would give her everything and enjoy her company, but she never seemed happy. I recall that my dad would often say that she could walk into the room and suck the joy right out of it, just by being there. There was a lot of hate and pain in his statement, but it did not entirely lack truth.

I honestly do not recall my mom ever enjoying life or expressing that she enjoyed life. Her beautiful face was a stone portrait. She was hardworking and determined. Outside of her looks, these were her best qualities. She would work two and three jobs, on top of going to college, to ensure we had housing and food. She may have been cold and unable to show me affection, but she did make sure that our very basic needs were met. She disliked driving and would walk everywhere. She eventually got her drivers' license in her late twenties or early thirties but would still choose to walk places if given the option.

I have a love of fitness, healthy eating and in general place a high value on healthy life choices. In a lot of ways, I think this stems from my mother and me observing her preferences. While she was very quiet and cold, she was passionate about eating right and the power of exercise.

As for her drug use, I don't think my mom was an addict. I think her drug use was more of a way to fit and blend in. I am no doctor, and I don't know my mother well at all, but if I had to guess, I would say that she suffered from depression and likely has trauma in her background as well. As you read this, you may be thinking that I did not grow up being raised by my mother, because I know so little about her, but sadly I was raised by her. She was there but not there.

She is a mystery to me. She would rarely speak to me and never about anything deep or emotional. There were two times she wrote me letters to help communicate her love and concern for me. I do not know her well enough to tell you much about her. I don't really know about how she grew up or what may have happened to her to make her the way she is. My dad shared with me that my mom was sexually abused, but at this point that is unconfirmed hearsay.

I do have a few fond memories of my mother, she was a wonderful cook and she made two dishes that I think about to this day; her spaghetti which was full of veggies and green chili pork burritos with homemade refried beans and charred flour tortillas. These dishes are my bittersweet comfort foods. She would also make homemade popcorn, the kind where you heat up oil on the stove and shake around the kernels, until they pop and spill over the lid. She would make popcorn and we would watch lifetime movies together, sitting in silence side-by-side. These memories are not much, but they are the good I hold on to. I love the taste of charred foods and popcorn is a comfort food that I often crave. I wonder if this is a mental comfort thing, that I gravitate towards without realizing it.

My mom is young, only 57 years old and I wonder if I would even recognize her if I passed her on the street. Outside of one negative in-person encounter, we have not exchanged more than a handful of Facebook messages in the past ten years. She is a phantom in my life. I know she is there, but I do not know her. I could not tell you where she works, how she spends her time, or if she thinks about me. This is a hurt that I choose, because I don't think I could weather more pain inflicted by her. I am choosing how I suffer, and not knowing her is the lesser of the two evils. In future chapters, I will discuss more about our dynamic and how we got here to this place of unknowing and distance.

My relationship with my mother has taught me a lot about what it is like to grieve a person who is still alive. In many ways, grieving the living is the harder form of grief, because the possibilities still physically exist, but they are not able to be made into a reality. When you are grieving someone that is still alive, you don't have the support system that often comes with physical death in the form of a funeral, a wake or other rituals performed to help us process the loss. When these rituals occur, we are often able to look back at the joy and highlights of that person's life. When you are grieving someone who is still alive, other people don't often understand, which is isolating. In many ways, I think our society prepares us to tolerate toxicity and abuse when that abuse occurs within families, and conditions us to believe that no matter what you should stand by your family. This mentality further isolates those that are in the painful position to grieve someone who is living ,or risk further damage or loss of themselves.

In general, I can sum up the "childhood" I had as a series of compound traumas, mixed in with some abuse and topped off with neglect. There were slivers of normality within the pain and sufferring. We lived at my great-grandparents' house on and off. When I was around five, we moved to an apartment forty-five minutes away from my great-grandparents. I have a few memories of this experience, the apartment had mice which caused me to suffer nightmares for years, that when I slept mice were crawling up my bed and into my hair; this is still an irrational fear I carry with me. The neighbors fed their kids, dry cat food on a regular basis- big, overflowing bowls of dry cat food with milk dripping down the sides of the bowl. I wonder how those kids turned out and if they recall their unusual breakfast with the revolt that I feel or was that simply part of their story. I struggle feeding my cat at times if my children are eating near the bowl of his food. It physically sickens me to think about feeding my children food intended for an animal. I can only imagine the desperation and love those neighbor parents must have felt for their children to make this horrendous choice.

I was sick and in the hospital a lot, which I didn't mind at all. The hospital was a safe and loving place where I was given everything I needed and cared for. It was around this time that I would daydream about being taken away from my parents to live in an orphanage or dream of being told that I was adopted, and my real family was coming for me. Sadly, this daydream carried me through some pretty dim nights when I didn't have the ability to muster the will to go to sleep knowing I would wake up to a harsh reality the next day. If I could trick my mind into thinking that tomorrow was the day I would be rescued, I would lull myself into a light slumber. I never enjoyed sleep and I learned to function on very little of it.

Relationships were not something I understood or had role models on. My mom was unable to be faithful to my dad, which caused a lot of turmoil in my household. At one point, my mom had yet another affair with a friend of my dad's and there was a big fight where a man was pushed through a wall in our apartment. If I am recalling it correctly, my dad was the aggressor, and the man was the man my mom was involved with. My dad was often crushed emotionally by the actions of my mother, but he always stayed around, and I never recall him threatening to leave her. This saddens me, that he did not have either the ability to stand up for himself or the ability to get the help that was needed to repair their marriage.

Another random and unusual childhood memory was us having poisonous black widow spiders, my dad kept in a jar on the coffee table as pets. People would come over and remark how cool this was. Now, I could see that being cool if the spiders were kept in terrariums or an insect habitat and not in empty pickle jars with the label partly torn off. It was during this time in our rundown apartment, where I was victimized by another family member. Walt, my original monster, sickness appears to have been genetic or perhaps this family member was another victim acting out what they had learned. I am not sure how long we lived in this apartment but it likely was not even a year before we were back at my Noni and Papa's house.

We remained at my Noni's house until one afternoon when I was eight, I got home from school that day and my mom said I had five minutes to grab "anything that was important to me" because we were "leaving and never coming back". My brother was a newborn baby at the time. We left and moved into a homeless shelter an hour away. Living in a homeless shelter was a huge change of pace. Any structure and security that I had felt or experienced was now fully gone.

When we were not in a shelter, we were couch surfing at my mom's "friends" houses. It was at one of these houses where I was victimized by a third person, a younger teen son of my mom's friend. At this home, there were a lot of people and very little space, so the adults felt it was best that this boy and I share a bed. Are you kidding me! These adults were either incredibly naive or incredibly irresponsible. He was fifteen or sixteen and I was eight.

So, by eight years old, I had been victimized more times than I could count, by three men, two of which I was related to and there was seemingly no light at the end of this very dark tunnel. I am thankful that I cannot recall what I thought and felt during these years. I was likely numb and just a shell of a little girl, pretty on the outside and hollow on the inside, pretending all was ok and putting one foot in front of the other each day.

At some point while I was still in elementary school, we stopped living in the homeless shelter/couch surfing scene in the Bay Area and graduated to living in the housing projects. At our first low-income apartment, which was a one-bedroom, ground floor apartment, my brother, mom and myself all shared the single bedroom. This lasted until our spot on the waitlist came up for a larger apartment. When we moved into the two-bedroom apartment, my mom and little brother shared a room, and I got my own bedroom which made me feel loved and special. It was "obvious" to me that my mom loved me more than my brother because she gave me the bedroom. I know that seems petty, but I was grasping at straws to find love and validation. It was the best I had felt in a long time.

The area that we moved into was culturally diverse and what I mean by that was, as a White girl, I was the minority. I LOVED the diversity. I was able to experience so many different cultures, backgrounds, and foods. That was the fun, exciting upside, the downside to living in this area was, I was bullied relentlessly and treated poorly for being different. People , and not just kids but adults too, automatically assumed that I thought I was better than them because I was White. If they only could see the emotional scars, physical internals battles , my lonliness, my pain, they would have seen that I didn;t identify as "white", I identified as "trash". I was a broken doll that may have been polished up to appear to be shiny and white but I was far from it. Looking back, I realize that I envied their struggles with race and discrimination, not because those were things they should have facing, not at all; I envivied that they were able to share and openly discuss their struggles while my struggles and shameful secrets had to remain hidden to avoid more pain and judgement.

If a boy showed interest in me, the other girls would tease and say, "oh they just like you because you are a weda". Weda or White girl was what they called me- I know, original right? Having red hair also meant that it was near impossible for me to just blend in and be a wallflower. I quickly learned that fear would not serve me well and I would have to be twice as tough to survive. So I was. I enhanced and fortified the invisible mask I wore to include strength and toughness, this outward exterior that made me appear bulletproof. I would not back down, yield to intimidation or otherwise let anyone fuck with me. I had years of pent-up anger and abuse to fuel this fire and I was burning white hot as I entered middle school. I know now, as a mom, all our kids go through mental preparations as they transition from elementary to middle school, but that is not what I am referring to. My mental preparedness was in essence an identity crisis in the making. I was being forced to be someone who I did not embrace, just to survive. I did not want to be tough. I wanted to be delicate, feminine, fun-loving, and easygoing. Looking back now, I see that this cocoon emersion experience was a theme that started long before this moment and it would be my cross to bear my entire life. To this day, there are times when I resent my strength, my fortitude and my independence. I feel that regardless of how hard I try to be soft and approachable, I come across as an intimidating and polished brute. I am an akward mix of power and femininity and I am often misunderstood before I even open my mouth to speak.

At school, I had always been a good kid. I was smart and school offered me a sense of stability that I did not experience at any other time or place. I loved school and truly embraced learning. I was able to be pretty much "normal" at school. I was a top performer, and I got a lot of praise and attention. I was also well liked by my peers and was popular. If you only looked at this facet of my life, these six hours, five days a week, my life would have seemed good, maybe even great at times. But just like any good story, there was a twist. Remember when those policemen visited my elementary school six years prior? Ya, well they told the school that I had been victim of sexual abuse by a family member and that little note was placed in my permanent school file.

In the state of California where I grew up, "troubled kids" were labeled as "601 kids". 601 kids were provided additional resources and support. As a 601 labeled kid, I was called down to the office a few months into my first year in middle school and I was spoken to about my "sexual history" and I was told all these supportive things the school would do for me. Man, they ruined it. They ruined my "normal" place. My safe place. The place where I did not have to live my regular life, I could live this alternate version which was so much better. I could not refuse their "help" or if I could, I did not know I could. I was put into this counseling group that met a few times a month to "celebrate our successes" and "process our feelings". So, a few times a month, I was pulled out of class where I was learning and thriving to connect with "troubled" kids who were making horrible choices in the present moment. This was not the "help" or exposure I needed.

Now, I had to figure out how to fit into this group I did not identify with and unfortunately, for most kids fitting in meant making choices which were not healthy or good for me. It was around this time that I split into a double life, good at school and into trouble at home. I really connected with the counselor for this 601 program, she was a younger woman, in her 20's, full of life, hope and naivete. She had not experienced one-one hundredth of the life me or any of these other kids had. Over the course of a few years, we grew close, and she would bring me to her house, about an hour from where I went to school, and we would spend weekends and school breaks together. It was great for awhile, I imgine it was like having an older sister. I know

now that it was not ok for her to bring me home to her house or to live with her part-time and she likely would have gotten into trouble had anyone found out. At the time, that never crossed my mind. She cared for me and that is what I focused on. Very few people had shown this level of caring for me and I was deperate for the feeling of acceptance.

About two years into our sister-like relationship, she got a serious boyfriend and they moved in together. She said, do not worry, he will love you and we will still be able to spend time together. Well, he loved me alright; he was abuser number four. Four abusers in about thirteen years, well wasn't I one lucky girl. I began to feel like I did not deserve this "normal" life that I saw all around me. I didn't fit in at school once people learned of my past and where I lived, the "bad" part of town in the low-income housing projects. At home, I was an outsider for the color of my skin, my hair color and my disinterest with drugs and alcohol which seemed to be a prerequisite for entry into friendships in my neighborhood. So, I did what any insecure, young teen girl without supervision and parents would do, I partied as best as I could, even though I hated the feeling of being drunk and high. I learned that I hated the feeling of loneliness more.

Chapter Three

HELLO MOTHERHOOD

My journey into motherhood began when I was fourteen years old. I had always been wise beyond my years or so I had thought. When my mother, brother, and I moved into the apartment after being homeless for some time, and me struggling to assimilate to my new neighborhood, I had finally begun making friends. One of my first friends was a boy my age, Christopher. Christopher was a middle child with an older brother, a younger brother and eventually a younger sister. We were neighbors and fast friends. Christopher's older brother, Jay, was the quintessential "bad boy". He was rebellious, dangerous, handsome and the boy everyone wanted, and I was instantly in love. The more time I spent around him, the more I wanted to be around him. He was an intense kid and always in trouble. Trouble with the law, trouble at school, trouble with other kids, if there was trouble to be found, he would find it. He was four years older than me and a wealth of worldly knowledge. I met him when I was nine years old and by the age of eleven, I was his. I word our relationship in this way because I was his possession. He treated me like he was my lord, and I was to do what he said and when he said it. As a young girl without parents or structure, I enjoyed this. It was a refreshing change, and I mistook his behavior as being true love. No one had ever "loved" me this much.

Jay and I never attended the same school as we were four years apart and to be honest, he rarely attended school, was kicked out of school several times, and eventually had to finish up at a continuation school. With him not being focused on school, he had a lot of time to focus on me and what I was doing and to control my experiences. Jay would hide in trees and observe me in secret, he would follow me around to see who I spoke to and for how long, he would come to my school and hide on rooftops and in other areas to monitor me. Later in our relationship when I moved into my first apartment, he would purchase spy-like audio equipment to listen to what was happening inside my apartment when I was home without him. He was "protecting" me if you asked him. While I didn't enjoy the constant monitoring, I got used to it and I rationalized that he would not go to these extremes if he did not really love me. Also, since there were so many other girls who were interested in him and I was the special girl he chose, I did not want to rock the boat and complain.

Being in a relationship with him made it very difficult to have friends, play sports, participate in school, and do many other "normal" things but again I was loved so the tradeoff was mostly worth it. Like any young person, I rebelled at times and I would sneak off to hang out with friends or stay after school to try out for a school play or for sports practice. These little acts of rebellion were mostly tolerated by Jay if there were no other boys or men around. He would grill me on what I did, who I spoke with, where I was and the gender of those who were there. Sometimes these conversations were tests as he had been monitoring me and already knew the answer and sometimes, he was just testing me to see if I would be honest.

Jay had a best friend who was much nicer than Jay. Keith was a free spirit and a different personality than Jay. I was really intrigued by these differences and I would enjoy the times we all hung out and I could talk more to Keith. In general, Jay had a large social circle, most being misfits, drug addicts, troublemakers and oftentimes criminals and so these people were also my people, even though I had nearly nothing in common with any of them. I was often alone in a room full of people.

I think at some point, I realized that Keith may be interested in being my friend. I was young and naive and misread some of his intentions. When Keith and I would hang out without Jay, because Jay was in jail ,or off with other girls (I was shocked and crushed when I learned we were not as exclusive as I thought), we would talk for hours and I felt like he really wanted to get to know me, my thoughts, and my feelings. This was a very different experience, and I grew to crave it, so I would hang out with him every chance I could. This went on for months and it was the one thing I kept from Jay. Deep down, I think I knew the risks, but it was worth it to have real conversations and feel a connection to another person.

One day, Jay showed up at my apartment door, where I lived with my mother and younger brother, and asked me to go for a walk with him. I felt a sense of unease that I had never felt before, but this was my boyfriend, my love, so I went without question. We walked down to the creek and under the overpass heading towards the river. As soon as we were out of sight, he began interrogating me. He was asking me questions about how I had been spending my time and who I was spending it with. My heart sank- he knew. I was guilty and he knew it, but at that moment, I did not know what to do, so I lied. I told half-truths and attempted to act normally. I will never forget what came next, this person that I loved, the person that I trusted more than anything, turned into a monster within seconds, right before my eyes. His face twisted and his words were nearly indistinguishable. That's when he hit me, as hard as I think he could right in my face, plunging his closed fist into my delicate, little girl face and he hit me again and again until I passed out.

I must not have been unconscious long, because I remember him picking me up and carrying me back towards the apartment community where we lived. I remember him carrying me to his apartment, where he lived with his mom, stepdad, and siblings. I heard him tell his mom that something happened to me, that I had fallen, and I needed a doctor. As they discussed what to do, I heard her repeatedly ask him what he had done to me and why. He just kept saying that I had fallen, and he may have accidently hit my head against his knee, when he went to help me. I can imagine that his clothes were bloody, his hands were likely torn up and his mother, knowing her son well, would have known better. They decided to not call an ambulance but rather, they loaded me into their station wagon and drove me to the local hospital. At the hospital, Jay's mother told the nurses and doctors that I had fallen, and I needed medical attention. During this time as I faded in and out of consciousness, Jay would lean down and whisper that he was sorry, and he did not mean it and to not tell anyone what had happened and that he loved me. He coached me as much as he could on this fictional story of my "fall".

Jay and his mother insisted on staying in the room with me while I was examined and when the doctor told them that they needed to wait in the hall for a moment, they protested. Eventually, the doctor cleared the room, so it was just him and I, and he asked me if Jay or someone else had hurt me. I remember thinking to myself that this was a big decision, I needed to decide right then and there what I wanted for my future, so I said in barely a whisper, "I fell by the river".

To describe my injuries better, the right side of my face was purple and extremely swollen to the point that I was not recognizable. I did not know it at the time, but the optic nerve in my right eye was permanently damaged and I would not see out of my right eye again for some time and even when my eye sight would return, it would not be fully restored. My nose was not broken but it was also severely injured, and my right cheek was fractured. It was clear from my injuries that I had not fallen.

The police were called, and Jay was arrested for assault. I was thirteen and Jay had just turned 18. These were not how I pictured us celebrating our milestone birthdays. Me in the hospital with signifigant injuries and he celebrating his intitial days as a legal adult from the confines of a jail cell. I refused to testify, I couldn't brign myself to be the reason Jay was in trouble again. Sickening to the version of me now, I would go to the jail every chance I could to visit him, reassure him that I did not get him in trouble and profess my undying love and commitment to him. I was a minor, so the only way I could get into the jail was with an adult. Jay's mom would take me to see him. She made the entire situation feel normal. Not once did she say anything negative about her son or his actions. This seemed like a part of adulthood that I was just being indoctrinated into, and not the horrific situation that it truly was.

I think Jay served a few months for what he did to me, but because I refused to testify, there was not anything more they could do. So, you may be questioning where my parents were in all of this and I am saddened to say they were nowhere to be found. My dad and mom had separated when she left him to move us into the homeless shelter and later they divorced. They were both actively in the throes of addiction and neither could be bothered with my troubles. My mom was aware of my relationship with Jay, as his mother had caught us in bed together at her house when I was 11 and he was 15 and confronted my mom. The only thing my mom said to me was, "I never want to see that woman at my house again". With my parents out of the picture Jay was all I had, and I was not about to lose him over my foolish choice to have friends, have male friends and not report to him my every move. I vowed to do better and treat him better. Yes, you read that right, I was going to treat him better. Ugh, looking back I want to shake myself and tell my younger self to snap out of it, run, and build a life without him. But I had no idea that was even an option. In my head, if I wanted love, he was the source of love and I needed to obey and comply to re-ceive that love. No one else in my life had ever loved me enough to set boundaries and try and protect me- these were the lines he fed to me that I would then repeat to myself to justify his ac-tions and keep me controlled.

At this point, after the assault, I was on the police's radar both because of my age, and his history of progressive crimes and also because a sheriff deputy was an older brother of a friend of mine.

This sheriff deputy was Jay's age and had grown up in our neighborhood but took a better path in life. After I was assaulted, there were times he was working at the jail when I went to visit, and he would refuse to allow me into the jail to see Jay. He tried to reason with me and tell me what a bad guy Jay was and to run as fast as I could away from him. Now, this man was credible for a moment, and nearly convinced me, until I attended a party while Jay was still in jail and he gave all of us underage kids alcohol and made sexual advances towards me. In that moment, I felt like Jay was right, there was no one I could trust, and he was right to protect me from these men who wanted nothing from me but sex. It also reinforced that there were no adults I could trust. It also began to shape that my self-worth was related to my sexuality and other's desire for me. I think it was at that moment or around that time of my life, approximately age thirteen that I saw that sex could be a form of currency whether that be social currency or actual currency. I shuddered at that idea, as I desperately just wanted to be loved and be this pure girl that Jay spoke of and expected. There was now a new added layer of complexity to my life, and I wanted no part of it.

Jay was released from jail around the time that my eyesight started to be restored in my right eye. It took about six months. During that time, the news of what really happened had travelled fast in our small area and my school counselor approached me about considering going to an alternative high school rather than starting my freshman year at the mainstream high school. He explained that he just felt I might be more comfortable at a school that offered me more flexibility. Mind you, I was a straight "A" student. I was mouthy, did drugs and drank alcohol, hung out with the wrong crowd, had a grown man for a boyfriend- who beat me, but I still deserved to be treated normally at school, so I refused. I let him know that I would be attending the normal high school.

I think in that moment, I was desperately crying out for help to be normal, to live a normal life. I knew that the path I was on was destructive, I did not want to be on that path, but I was not sure what to do about it. I did know that if I gave up going to a normal high school, I would be straying even further from the ability to live differently. I felt like school was my only hope for a better future.

It was the summer before I started high school when another plot twist occurred in my life. My mother, whom I still lived with, decided she would be getting remarried, and she and my younger brother would be moving in with her new husband. This new husband was not a stranger to me, not at all. He was my dad's high school best friend and someone I had known all my life. My mother explained that they wanted an opportunity to have a family and because of my choices, they felt it would be best that I do not move with them. That is right, at thirteen, I was officially given a pseudo eviction notice by my mother and told to move and figure it out. This sent me into a tailspin of sorts, I was devastated. How could my mother just decide that she was going to be clean, live as a productive member of society and start a new family without me. I felt so alone, abandoned, and trashy. I acted out a bit, got in even deeper with the wrong crowd, experienced homelessness again, and felt my life spiraling out of control. I cannot recall where I heard about emancipation, but I think it was from a social worker at the homeless shelter. I thought, well I have been on my own basically my entire life, so why not make it official, that I would be an adult and be able to work and support myself.

At thirteen, I officially began the process of becoming

emancipated. The start of the process involved meeting with a judge. When I first met with the judge, before I could even say a word, he said that he would never sign off on an emancipation for someone so young. He explained that there is a process that I will need to go through which includes meeting with a court social worker, a child psychologist, finding a job and showing that I would have the means to support myself, among other hoops. He stated that once this process is completed, he would review the reports and meet with me to reveal his final decision. We met again five months later. When I think of the conversation, I still tear up. The judge said that he wanted to thank me. Thank me, for opening his eyes and showing him that he cannot stereotype people for any reason, especially for being young. He said he was incredibly impressed by me and that there was not a single person who had met with me, that would not support my emancipation. He said it was clear to them all, that I was a special girl and that they were all so proud of me. Proud of me! They were proud of me. Cue the victory music, I the girl who had been nothing so far in my life made someone proud. Not because I studied and got an A, but me as a person, impressed another human being and they were proud. Wow, this changed my life. Those small words of encouragement gave me hope for the first time in my young life. I had no idea what the path could be, but I felt that I could survive and be happy.

Towards the end of the emancipation process, I moved into Jay's mother's house, which was a two-bedroom apartment that was already full of people and dysfunction, but it was a place to live. Jay and I slept on the living room floor together each night and there was rarely enough food for all of us, so I learned to be comfortable in a constant state of discomfort. I was also still struggling with my eyesight and was too afraid to say anything, so I just learned to live with it even though I could barely see things that were directly in front of my face, especially out of my right eye. Since Jay and I lived together, he expected that I would behave like a wife to him every day. This consisted of doing what he said, having sex multiple times a day even though there was no privacy or private space. This resulted in my feeling humiliated, shamed, and embarrassed every day of my life.

Jay did not work as he could not hold down a job given his criminal record, poor attitude and drug use. I was working very part-time as a reading fluency teacher and attending my freshman year of high school full-time. We heard daily from Jay's mom both directly and indirectly that we were a burden. I was on the list to get my own income-based apartment, but I knew the waiting list was long. Feeling like a burden and struggling to handle Jay's mood swings and drug use, I decided to try and move in with my dad who lived an hour away.

My dad was newly remarried and were expecting a baby and from what I could see, he appeared to be the most stable that he had ever been. He was clean and sober and working. I do not have anything bad to say about my experience living with him, only that it was very brief, and my dad and his wife had struggles surrounding being a blended family. She had two children from a previous relationship and was pregnant with a child they would share together. About a week after moving in with him, I was not feeling well, so I went to a local, free health clinic. I found out that day that I was pregnant. Pregnant at fourteen.

I was confused but overjoyed at being pregnant. I had not ever thought about having children or a family of my own, but I embraced it. When people, including my mother, told me to have an abortion, I shot them down saying that I knew that this was a potential consequence to having sex and I was going to take care of my child. The pregnancy pushed Jay and I back together. Had I not gotten pregnant, me moving to live with my dad would have ended our connection and allowed both of us to move on with our lives. I moved back in with him at his mother's house and I grew very close to his mother. She was excited to be a grandmother.

My pregnancy was uneventful, I doubled up on classes at school and began attending college classes in addition to high school classes. I was happy, my life felt pretty stable and I felt

I was on a forward trajectory. Jay was on his best behavior and even managed to get a job and keep it for the months leading up to the birth of our son. We got engaged and were planning our wedding. Life was beginning to feel comfortable. It was not traditional but it felt like a skewed version of what I had seen on TV and read in books.

I gave birth that August to a beautiful baby boy. I was so in love. Jay's mom and Jay both were with me when I gave birth and were equally as smitten with the baby. My family didn't come to the hospital to see me and didn't meet my son until he was a month old or so. I barely even noticed their lack of interest as I was happy for the first time in my life.

My mom did start coming around, about the time I was getting married, and my son was three months old. Jay and his family were Mormon and while Jay attended seminary, he had been kicked out of that too, but his mom insisted we be married in their church. I had no religious background or understanding so it sounded fine by me. To be married in their church, I needed to meet with their religious leader and answer some questions. I do not recall all the questions but there was one that stood out to me. They asked me if I had ever had a "lesbian encounter". Being the unknowledgeable and feisty girl I was, I joked and asked if that is anything like an alien encounter, because I have had a few of those. They were not amused by my humor, but they gave us the blessing we needed to proceed. A few days before the wedding, we needed to meet with a judge to obtain our marriage license. While I was legally emancipated, I was still underage. So, we met with the judge and he signed off on the license.

I had never been the kind of little girl to dream of a wedding or even a marriage, my upbringing did not allow for the extravagance of having dreams. I just merely was surviving and focused on what it took to do so. But I let my guard down and was excited for the wedding we had planned. I had a beautiful dress, a woman who volunteered with teen moms let me borrow, my closest girlfriends were my bridesmaids and even the wedding cake, with the figure of a man and women on top meant that I would have a normal wedding.

This was it; this was the start to my "normal" life, and I was ready. Imagine my shock and disappointment when thirty minutes after the ceremony was supposed to begin Jay's mom came in and told me that Jay was not coming. She said with a plain face that he didn't want to marry me. I did not understand how that could be, I had just seen him the night before and he was in love with me and we were on our path to happiness, all our friends and family were there; just outside the door where I stood and sobbed. What was I going to do, this was my plan, this was my "normal" and everyone was going to see that I wasn't "normal" and that I was not loved.

What I feared was, I was not lovable and that was the real reason he did not show up. This was another crossroads in my life, and I had moments to decide what to do. At that moment, I refused to be a victim. I was lost but I would not be broken.

I went into the chapel and let everyone know that there would be no wedding that day but that they were all invited to join me in the reception hall to celebrate life. I spent that night dancing, eating and celebrating with every one that meant something to me. I wore something new that day, that would stay a part of me for many years to come. I wore a mask, a disguise. From that day on, I had a public face that was strong, fierce, determined, unaffected and beautiful. That would be the person the world would see. I would no longer show anyone the lost, victimized, abandoned, trashy, and vulnerable girl who was really living inside me.

Coincidently, the day after my failed attempt at a marriage, the low-income apartment complex called to tell me that there was an apartment available for me and I could move in, in two-weeks and based on my income, my rent would be $8 a month. On December first, at the age of 15, before I was even old enough to drive or have my learners permit, I moved into my first apartment. I felt like a real adult and my life was starting to take shape. I may not have had much, but I was determined to give my son and I a good life.

Jay did not like that I was comfortable with my independence and he weaseled his way back into my life again and again. He would show up, want to control me, and tell me what to do, maybe see his son for a few minutes, have sex and then move on. He was still important to me, but we could both tell that he was losing his grip on my life and I was maturing. Over the course of that next year, we would make up and break up more times than I could count. Any length of time I did not hear from him, he was either in jail or pursuing a relationship with other young girls. I quickly realized that there was a pattern and he liked young women, like middle school and early high school aged girls, even those he was nearly twenty-one years old. My heart was broken, but I was moving on. I was too afraid to chance getting into another relationship for fear of retaliation from Jay, and life had taught me that relationships hold no positive value. I was better off alone.

Being a mother was tough and being a single parent in high school was a huge challenge even for someone as determined as I was. I struggled to keep up with work, school, and motherhood. I had very little idea of what I was doing, and learning as I went was a tough strategy, but I was doing it. I felt happy and I was even seeing and hearing more and more from my mother. It seemed that becoming a mother would be what bridged the gap between us. On New Year's Eve, the year I turned sixteen, my mom offered to babysit so I could go to a party with my friends. I was attending the party with Jay's brother, the brother who I had been close friends with. We had a platonic friendship and he invited me out to this party with his friends. I was excited to go since ,for about a year, I had been solely focused on raising my son, working, and going to school, and felt it would be nice to have a night out to be able to feel like a teen.

The first part of the night went well, my son was at my mom's house, Christopher picked me up and we went to the party. It was a low-key environment and we mainly chatted and danced until midnight. Shortly after midnight, Christopher drove me home and dropped me off in the parking lot in front of my apartment. I went inside and remember feeling excited to have a night to myself to do whatever I wanted, watch tv, eat a late-night snack and sleep in the next morning, all things I no longer did as a mother.

I entered my apartment and threw my keys on the table, slipped off my coat and walked toward the bedrooms, which were down a narrow hallway at the back of the apartment. I passed my son's room, and the door was open, this was normal as I had this weird thing about closed doors. I am claustrophobic so even normal sized rooms, when doors were closed, freaked me out. As I walked past his room, I had a strange feeling, but I shook it off and attributed it to having not been alone in my apartment for over a year. I went into my bedroom and started to grab my pajamas, and something occurred to me, when I had walked past my son's room the closet door was closed. This was not normal as I never closed the closet doors. He wasn't fully mobile so there was little possibility that he had slid it shut before we left, but my mother might have, either way it was bugging me.

I went into his room and flipped on the light, that feeling of fear and anticipation welled up in my throat. I remember thinking that I was being silly and freaking myself out for no reason. I put my hand on the closet door and slowly slid it open, what I saw did not register in my mind immediately. There was a pile of unfolded clothes and blankets on the floor of the closet, and I had not recalled leaving it like that. I started to bend down to pick them up to see what it even was and that is when I saw it, skin, a forearm was in the clothes. Before I could pull my thoughts together, Jay jumped up from out of the pile of clothes and I started running. I ran for the kitchen where the phone was. The apartment was small, and he was right behind me. As soon as I got to the phone, he grabbed me and pushed me to the ground. He grabbed the phone and yanked it hard out of the wall. That is when I saw what was in his hand, an aluminum bat. He struck me with the bat as he was yelling at me and interrogating me about where I had been and what I had been doing. He accused me of all sorts of things and was in such a rage, I could barely understand what he was saying. I gathered that he was mad that I went out and that his son at my mother's house and that I was out with his brother. I tried to explain but he was unwilling to listen. I felt like I had to get out of the apartment as I felt that had I stayed he would kill me.

I made a few attempts to get to the door and get it unlocked. We were physically fighting, and I was unwilling to give up. On about the fourth attempt, I managed to get the door unlocked and opened. I was barefoot and still in my glittery party dress; I was bleeding from my head and face and I was crying so hard I could barely see. It was raining hard that night, the rain was coming down in sideways sheets, and the apartment complex was eerily quiet. I ran as fast and as far as I could, banging on every door I passed, screaming for help. I was trying to get anyone to let me inside and several people refused and shut their doors. I was hiding in the bushes trying to silently catch my breath and figure out where to go, when I heard music and talking. I then saw Jay coming in my direction, so I bolted towards the music. There were a few people, a woman and two men standing on a low balcony of an apartment. I ran towards them screaming for help, using every ounce of energy I had to gain their attention. The rain and the music made it impossible for them to hear me until I was right up close to them. I could only manage to say, "he is going to kill me" before I collapsed. Luckily, the men came down and kept Jay from me while the woman called the police. She happened to be a mom of a girl I knew from school and she recognized me. Jay had run off when the police sirens were approaching and was not arrested for a few days. My injuries were minor in comparison to the first time he hit me. I was physically ok, nothing was broken, I was swollen and bloody but mentally I was a mess. I was terrified and traumatized.

The police connected me with a victim advocate to help me navigate the legal system, to include attending counseling paid for by the state for trauma victims, to prepare to testify at the trial and in general be a support while I processed what I had went through. Not just the recent physical attack, but the five years of abuse I had experienced in various forms. I was so confused, I still loved him, but I was terrified of him. I did not have a support system really, his family immediately took his side and blamed me for all his behavior and struggles. My mom blamed me and said that I should have never gotten involved with him and look at what I did to myself. I started to believe them all. I thought that this was my fault and that I had screwed up our lives. I even began to question if he had actually abused me or if I had imagined the physical abuse and stalking. The common denominator in all the abuse I had suffered since birth was me; so it must be me that was the problem. I internalized my experiences and began to hate myself.

I went through another phase of grief where I was angry at Jay for leaving me and being put in jail and later in prison for what he had done to me. The courts provided a lot of tangible support. This was a monumental case for them, they said. It would be the first time they were prosecuting someone for corporal injury to a spouse, when the perpetrator was not married to their victim. This was a much higher charge than the previous charge of assault. The charge had the potential of putting him in prison for a significant amount of time.

I struggled to testify at the trial, I had a lot of pressure internally and externally to not testify but I did it anyways, even though I did not want to. There is even part of me to this day where I question if I ruined his life by testifying against him. Was I the reason he would not lead a normal life? This still haunts me. Part of me sees him as the predator and part of me sees that person that I loved and feels he was just a misguided kid just like me. An abused mind is not a clear mind and at this point in my life, I was swimming in pool of unresolved traumas. I could not make heads or tails of my life and I was equally numb and deeply wounded.

Jay went to prison and I believe has been out and back into prison a few times since this trial, and the charges related to his abuse of me. In the past twenty years, I lost contact with him. There were some years early on, when I would write to him and once when he was out on parole, I ran into him and we hung out for a while. There was so much pain between us, but the anger and fear had subsided. When he wasn't actively abusing me, his presence was the most comforting part of my life. He was where I felt at home. I am not sure what has become of his life, but I wish him the best and wherever he is, I hope he found his happiness and peace.

While I was processing the abuse and separating from my abuser, unknowingly rekindling a relationship with my mother would change my life forever. It would seem that I was jumping out of one frying pan and into the fire. While she was "helping" me with my son ,while I went to counseling, attended school, and continued working on and building my life. My mother was cooking up her own plans. Seeing that my guard was down, she used my time of weakness against me. She went to the courts and told them that I was an unfit mother and convinced them that she should have custody of my son.

Given the history of abuse, my age, and her now good standing with the community, the courts agreed. Without my input, appearance, or involvement, they gave her temporary guardianship of my son. Now, I am sure she has her own version of the story and she will say that she was just looking out for what was best for us both, but she will forever in my mind be a liar and a kidnapper. What I had heard was that her new husband and she wanted more children, but my mother was unable to have more children, so they decided to take mine. It sounds crazy and farfetched, as a mother myself it is unfathomable that someone would treat their child the way my mother treated me, but she did.

I have very few regrets in my life, but not being able to raise my firstborn son in the way I wanted to will always haunt me. In some ways, it would define me for many years and prevent me from being a mother at all. Now, I want to explain, I did not go down without a fight. I was sixteen years old, had no family, no support, my son's father was in jail for beating me and he would be in prison for years to come, I had a tenth-grade education, no money to speak of, a troubled reputation and a sassy and bold attitude. I was not able to fight fair, so I did the only thing I could think of. I took him back.

I showed up at the daycare where they enrolled him, and he was outside playing in the yard. My little redheaded, round cheeked, toddler was playing happily with a group of kids. I went up to the fence, reached over, grabbed him, and walked away.

I was later arrested for this act of motherly love. The charges didn't stick, but my mother was able to use my act of love to show my instability and immaturity. This would be used as a basis of the decision to grant my mother and her husband guardianship. The same court who three years earlier emancipated me because my parents were unfit and I was caring for myself, just gave that same woman my son. Our court system is irrevocably broken. I don't have a relationship with my mother, and she has portrayed me and the situation in a way that caused damage to the relationship between my son and myself. I refuse to fight in that same way and damage my son's relationship with my mother. To do so now, would be cruel and would leave him with a similar hole in his heart.

I pray every day that God will restore our relationship now that my son is a grown man with a family of his own. There are some hurts that are so deep that they can only be healed by God and for me this is something I place lovingly in His hands. Whether our relationship is restored, or God heals us separately, I trust that this experience will be worked into good, because that is what my God does, he turns the hurts into victories and the troubles into glory.

Chapter Four

MARRIAGE CONFORMITY

After losing custody of my son and being free of the dysfunctional love I found in my abusive boyfriend, I was more lost and lonelier than I had ever been. I wasn't sure what to do. I was just about to graduate from high school, two years early, thanks to my hard work. I felt like my life was over. I had worked so hard and everything I worked for had been taken from me in a matter of weeks. I would sit in my empty apartment, surrounded by my son's things and I would just cry and cry. I could barely function, and I sunk into a dark place mentally and emotionally.

I once again fell in with the wrong crowd. They hadn't gone far, and they seemed to welcome me with open arms, the moment my life fell apart. I found comfort in other lost souls who had nothing to live for and nothing to lose. I was partying a lot. Drinking vodka shots from large teacups like some sort of Alice in Wonderland tea party guest. Anything I could do to numb the pain. One night, I was throwing an impromptu party at my apartment. Think loud music, inappropriateness, a lack of respect, drugs and all the other things that this lifestyle brings. A new neighbor moved into the apartment above me. A younger guy, maybe in his early twenties. He came down to ask us to keep the noise down, as he had to work the next day. I was thinking at the time that this guy was so lame. He was young, he should be partying with us.

We settled down the best we could, but likely we were still loud and obnoxious. When I sobered up the next day, well sobered up enough to leave the apartment, I ran into him and I curtly apologized, bracing myself for a lecture, but he did not lecture me. Later that night he came downstairs to my apartment and we started what would be an insightful and prodigious friendship. He was older than I thought, twenty-seven, and he had this chill and laid-back way about him. We chatted about philosophy and life, deep conversations and we would talk for hours.

Instead of hanging out with the party crowd, I would make excuses to stay home in hopes that we would get to chat. We had this secret code, where we would tap on the ceiling back and forth to indicate if we were free to talk. Hey, don't laugh this was way before cell phones and this was like our version of an instant message. Did I mention that all these chats usually occurred while laying next to each other in either his bed or mine?

Yes, and not once did Jason make a move on me or make me feel even the slightest bit uncomfortable. Our friendship continued to grow and develop over the course of about five months. I cared so deeply for him, not an infatuation or lust, it was something that I had never experienced before. Maybe this was what real friendship looked like. Well, whatever it was, it changed me. It opened my eyes to a new way of thinking. I was reinvigorated with a new passion to learn and succeed. I was excelling in school for the first time in a long time, and I was feeling like an improved version of myself.

Our neighbor talks tapered off some, as I focused on school. I realized a few days went by and we had not connected. I took out the green handled, yellow straw broom and I tapped on the ceiling but would get no response even when I saw his lights were on. I continued this for days and still no response. I was beginning to feel rejected and abandoned. Where was my friend, I needed him and his wisdom? It was the fuel my soul needed to continue this transformation that I had just begun. One night about a week later, I heard tapping, but I was pissed at what I would now describe as a feeling of rejection, so I laid silently in bed in protest.

A few days later, I came home from class and the apartment maintenance guys were working in Jason's apartment. They had paint and rollers and buckets. I could tell that it was not a small work order they were there for. I went up to them and out of character for me, demanded to know what they were doing in that apartment. Stunned by my tone, one maintenance man replied in his broken English, that nobody lives there. I responded that yes, Jason does. He then looked at me with the saddest, most caring brown eyes and said "no, hunny, he die". My heart sank, this could not be true. I finally made a friend, and he died, no way, this could not be true! What I later learned was that Jason went out for a night of drinking for his birthday, with his dad and brother, and while at the bar he tripped and fell. He went home and was fine it seemed, he awoke the next morning and complained to his brother that he had the worst hangover and would be calling in and taking it easy that day. They think he died later that day.

It was a brain aneurysm which was triggered by his fall the night before. He was upstairs in his apartment directly above me, while I stewed and pouted about him ignoring me, rejecting me, and abandoning me, all while he was dead or dying. That fucked me up for a long time. Both the grief from the loss and the wondering, if instead of pouting and fretting, I would have gone up there and just checked on him, would that have made a difference. I even went through a time where I thought I had imagined the entire friendship and questioned my own sanity. While our friendship was short and ended tragically, he was perhaps the most positively impactful person thus far in my young life.

I was so scarred from his passing, that I had to move for my own mental health's sake. I would hear what I thought was him tapping to communicate with me for weeks and it made me feel unsettled and crazy. This pushed me to contemplate big changes in my life.

I had graduated high school and my classes at the junior college had ended. I wanted to move to the city and attend a university, but I was broke. I had an old car, some tattered furniture, a little bit of clothes and about $500 in the bank. I was determined to make the move, but a path to do so seemed unclear and arduous.

My grandmother, the hairbrush yielding grandmother, lived just outside of the city I wanted to move to, so I gave her a call and explained what I wanted to do and asked if she would let me stay there. I had been hearing about how well she was doing and thought perhaps she was now medicated. She had taken learning a new language very seriously and had immersed herself in the Hispanic culture. Her entire life now revolved around her new focus. My family would joke that she was a "born again Hispanic" rather than a "born again Christian". Nothing my family did seemed normal. She said, "sure, I will rent you a room" and we agreed on $300 a month for one bedroom in her small apartment. I moved in the next week. I paid her $300 and rationed the remaining $200 for food and gas to get me by until my student aid came through.

Within a month, I was attending classes and living with my grandmother. When the first of the month rolled around, my grandma asked me about the $300 for the month, and I explained that I was just waiting on my financial aid to come through, which was expected later that week. She told me that she was fine waiting but would charge me a $50 late fee for the inconvenience to her. I didn't want to argue so I agreed to pay the $50. My grandmother was a hoarder of clothes and shoes, her entire apartment was packed full of these items and she had storage sheds off-site, also full of clothing and shoes.

The little room I was renting was full of her items and I had just enough space to have a twin bed and nightstand. I would sit on my bed to study and would use the nightstand as a makeshift bookshelf. There was no place for me to put my clothes, even underneath the twin bed was taken up by her clothes and shoes. My clothes and personal items were in bags which I would use as pillows on my bed. Actually, every square inch of the house was covered with stuff, she was a full-blown hoarder.

I knew the relationship was fragile so I never complained and did whatever I could to keep the peace. As agreed, Friday came, and I cashed my check and gave grandma $350. I then left for school.

I was just about to school when I was pulled over by a police car. The policeman approached my car with his gun drawn, which I found to be really odd since I hadn't done anything. He yelled at me to show my hands and step out of the vehicle. I asked if he could tell me what I had done and what this was about. He ignored my requests. He then handcuffed me and sat me on the curb while he went and searched my car. I was thinking to myself that this was just a mistake, and if I stayed calm it would be over soon and we would be laughing about the mistaken identity. After searching my car and finding nothing, the officer came back over to me and had a female officer come and search me. They also pulled up my sleeves and gave my body a once over. Now, I was thoroughly confused.

After what I could only imagine was a satisfactory search, the male officer asked me where I was headed, and I responded to school and named the school. He then asked me if I knew a woman by the name of and then proceeded to say my grandmothers' name. I replied yes and that she is my grandma. Long story short, after kissing me goodbye and telling me to have a great night at school, my grandma called the police and reported that I pushed her down and stole her pain medication, and my behavior was due to heroin withdrawals. WHAT!?! I had not touched her, and I had never done heroin. Luckily, the police realized that something wasn't right about her story and they let me go but told me not to return to my grandmother's house or to contact her. No problem, sir. I could guarantee with extreme certainty that I would not contact her again.

So here I was with nothing, no money, all of my material belongings were now taken from me, no place to live, nothing to eat, no money and no family; I was once again lost. But I refused to give up. I had a car and I learned to live in my car. I learned where I could park, where I would be safe and not be bothered. I went to class when I had class, I worked two or more jobs at any given time. I was doing all that I could to survive. I still didn't have much money as I was carrying a heavy load at school which meant I only worked about 20-30 hours a week, at minimum wage. Living in one of the most expensive areas of the country, this was not going to get me much.

I was saving money by eating free food provided at work as a perk, and at video stores on their themed nights. Some nights at the video store, dinner was popcorn and on the lucky nights I might score a free hotdog or taco. I never could afford to rent a movie, not to mention I didn't own a tv or have a place to watch one, but I browsed the shelves so I wouldn't look suspicious. I think in hindsight, the staff knew I was only there for the food and they took mercy on me.

I joined a gym that had showers and low monthly fee ,so I could shower regularly and watch tv while I worked out. I would write my papers for school at the laundromat while I washed my clothes because there was space to sit, and I could use the tables as a makeshift desk. I was happy living this simple life. It became increasingly harder to find places to park at night to sleep, so I started parking at work, at my manufacturing plant, swing-shift job and sleeping there after my shift. Until one night when my boss, a man in his late twenties confronted me. I was humiliated and tried to lie. I claimed I had been drinking and did not feel safe to drive. He saw right through me. I was as straight-laced ,at this point, as they come, and I didn't drink or do any drugs.

He took me home with him and introduced me to his landlord Susan, who rented out rooms in her house to students. She was a Jewish widow and a real free-spirit. She had this flowy, salt and pepper hair that was styled like a young Farrah Fawcett. She wore long peasant skirts in bright and fun patterns, with a t-shirt and Birkenstocks every day.

She cooked meals for us, served family style,and made us all sit around the table and talk. I loved living there. It felt like I was finally part of a community. During one of the family meals, Suzanne had cooked an Indian dish using chicken thighs and all sorts of exotic and fragrant spices. I sat down to eat with our little makeshift family about 11pm one night. I appreciated that while we loosely had a family dynamic, we were anything but traditional. I was starving that night as I still didn't have much money for food and these home cooked meals were a real treat after primarily living off bagels and popcorn. I was on my second bowl of this stew-like chicken dish when I felt this strange sensation when I swallowed. It almost felt like my throat was being cut as the food went down. I kept trying to clear my throat and stay calm. I said to Suzanne that I wasn't feeling well and explained to her what the sensation was. At that moment one of the other roommates pulls a small chicken bone from his bowl.

I knew instantly that I had swallowed a bone and it was stuck. I could feel this tightening sensation almost like a balloon was blowing up in my chest and throat. Suzanne grabbed her coat, we piled in her Honda Civic and drove to the nearest emergency room. Like typical nights in an ER waiting room there were lots of people and I was walking, talking and not bleeding out, so they deemed me to not be a priority. At one point when I was complaining of my symptoms worsening, they pulled Suzanne aside and said that I was likely just having a panic attack, and when I had swallowed the food made a strange sensation as it went down, and my mind was blowing it out of proportion. They gave me a valium and had us sit for another few hours while they waited for a doctor to see me. About two hours later, a man dressed in scrubs ,called my name from an open swinging door. I walked over to him in pain, but less panicked thanks ot the valium, and he explained that he was from Radiology and that he would be taking me down to X-ray for some images. As I got into a gown and laid down on the metal x-ray table, I began to doubt myself.

Maybe I was just having a panic attack, maybe they were right, and I was fine and just making a big deal over nothing. I had nearly convinced myself of their truth when after taking two images the technician bolted from the room. I mean this guy was moving fast. Now, maybe it was the valium or maybe it was my lack of medical industry knowledge, but his actions did not frighten me. I think I thought he just had to go somewhere in a hurry. Imagine my surprise when he came running back in with a handful of medical professions trailing behind him.

There were nurses starting IV's and nurses on the phone making some kind of arrangements. A doctor knelt down to me and with such a kindness to his voice asked me "how are you doing". When I attempted to respond, there was a sharp pain in my throat that cut off my words. My lips were moving but the sound would not quite come out. The doctor explained that the x-rays revealed that the chicken bone that I thought I swallowed had lodged itself and perforated my esophagus causing swelling in my throat and chest which was what was creating my discomfort. Moments after his words registered in my mind, I had lost consciousness. I am not sure if they gave me something in the IV or I simply just gave in to the pain. I woke up the next day in a hospital bed. It was explained to me that they had removed the bone ,and repaired me the best they could, but it was unknown what, if any ,long-term effects I would experience. The long term effects that they were unsure of, would turn out to be extremely significant impediment in my future quality of life.

The damage caused my muscles to not work consistently or correctly. Now when I swallow, I never know if the food and drink will go down smoothly, or if the muscles will spasm and seize and hold my food hostage in the throat until it releases. I had to learn to eat for worst-case scenario, which means that I no longer eat solid foods- no dense meat, bread, large bites, anything irritating, basically I watch every bite of food extremely closely. It has been over two decades now since the injury and I suffer from depression and shame in every bite. I am self-conscious when I have to eat in front of anyone that is not in my immediate family. I often have to cough my food back up when it gets stuck, drink hot drinks to relax the muscles to allow food to pass easily and I can only successfully swallow about a tenth of what I need to feel full and satisfied. I would have thought that this would make me incredibly thin, but in fact I battle with my weight because I suffer from such poor nutrition. I learned to rely on sugar and sweetened dairy as a quick fix to my low energy.

Under times of stress, my muscles work even worse than ever which means that I go between starving myself out of fear of choking or I binge eat items like milkshakes just to feel like I have enough food to survive. This pattern extrapolated over two decades has wrecked my mental and physical health. There are times that I am a warrior, willing to do whatever it takes to fill body my body with as much nutrient dense, clean, pureed, and thin foods I can get my hands on but often, I reduce myself to eating lots of dairy and chewing up and spitting out foods just to experience their flavor.

I am always sucking on menthol cough drops to keep the esophageal spasms to a minimum and I always have lots of liquids on hand to keep my throat lubricated and calm. This is a dark truth that I hide from the world because I fear that people will not understand or relate. I cannot even eat like a normal person- how alienating when our culture is so driven and communal when it comes to food. There's definitely been a theme in my life of having this idea of what a normal life should be and feeling that I am not living that life.

What I would not realize for years to come, and it may be what is holding you back too, is that the feeling that I was desiring, came from within me. I had to accept that my life, as messy, as complicated, and as troubled as it was, was the exact thing that would make me the strong, determined and independent woman I was on the cusp of becoming.

As I sat in a pool of my own pity about my swallowing disorder, I sank into yet another deep depression. I stopped attending classes, I went on disability, and I gave up on my life. I slowly started finding comfort in old behaviors. I went out a lot, partied but stayed sober around others who weren't sober ,and I refused to focus on the good in my life.

Around this time, my California Victim of Crime court appointed advocate reached out to check on me and let me know that my abuser was being transferred to a new facility. She mentioned that she noticed I had not used much of my victims of crime money which I was provided by the state to help me overcome my abuse and trauma. I mentioned that I had tried counseling and it just wasn't helpful. This was truly how I felt. I had attended counseling and I felt it was this person who knew very little about me pitying me and judging me. Giving me advice and ideas from a perspective they could not possibly ever relate to or understand. After a handful of sessions, I decided my time was best used elsewhere. There was something in me, coming from a place of desperation that felt the lifeline of hope, this advocate was throwing me. She offered to find me a counselor who might be a better fit in the town that I was living in, and for whatever reason I agreed.

A week later, I was in my first counseling session with a middle-aged woman named Anne. Anne had a vintage looking office in a historic downtown building, that was once a house. The porch creaked loudly as I walked up the steps to the antique looking door. Inside the office smelled slightly musty ,but it was decorated in this eclectic mix of modern and thifty finds. I took a seat on the oversized blue couch and proceeded to tell my story of eighteen years of unfair hardships. I gave just enough detail to make me feel uncomfortably vulnerable, but not so much that I would not be able to look this woman in the eye if I chose to come back for a future session. I recall Anne listening intently with a very blank look on her face, in hindsight this demeanor helped me feel comfortable and not feel threatened. I spoke for a full two hours after which Anne thanked me and asked if I wanted to come back next week. I kind of did, so I made another appointment.

Now this counseling session was distinctly different,

Anne had not asked me a single question after our introduction until she asked me at the end if I wanted to return. If this is a trained counseling tactic, I would not have known. Her almost lack of interest, interested me. I could tell from her body language that she had been listening, the look on her face was kind, passive and nonjudgmental but she did not pry.

She did not make me uncomfortable and because of that I returned, not thinking I would learn anything or be healed in any way, but I knew instinctively I would be heard. I continued seeing Anne for a few months and I would pour my heart out about whatever was going on in my life, my thoughts on my past, basically whatever I wanted to talk about. After six or so sessions, I felt like I didn't have much else to say and Anne rarely said much so I felt like our relationship was nearing the end.

That is when she surprised me. About 20 minutes into my hour-long session, Anne interrupted me. Mid-sentence she said can I stop you there. Shocked, I just looked at her. She took my silence as permission to continue. She looked me right in my eyes and said, "in life you have two choices, you can choose to be right, or you can choose to be happy, but you cannot choose both at the same time". Ok- so what? Why are you telling me this, I replied with clear irritation in my voice?

Her response would change the way I looked at my life.

She continued to say that she has now listened to me for roughly 10.5 hours and it is clear that I am angry and upset at what has happened to me in my young life, and she said "you have every right to be angry, hurt, discouraged, upset, you name the emotion and you have the right to feel all of those things and likely more, but you are choosing to be right when I hear that you so desperately want to be happy". It took me a moment to process what she was insinuating. She was saying that I was my own problem. She was telling me that I was choosing to be miserable and waste my life away, and the power and choice was mine.

Well, I responded in the only way I could in my immature and emotionally stunted vocabulary, I stood up, looked her straight in her eyes and said, "fuck you, you know nothing about me" and I stomped out, and slammed that fancy, antique door of hers so hard I thought the glass would shatter.

I went home and went on with my life stewing and focusing on the stupid things Anne-who knows nothing- said to me. That little seed that Anne planted was growing in me. Every time I caught myself having a negative thought or emotion, I would catch myself saying in a silly and mocking tone, "Angela, you have a choice you can be right, or you can be happy". I slowly started shifting my routine choices to be more choices of conscious thought.

I learned that I had power over my thoughts and with that power, I slowly began choosing to make a life for myself. You see, up until this point I was either pitied or used; I would survive whatever showed up in my path and I would get through it and continue. Life was happening TO me and I was a passive participant in many ways. I began to explore and test what life would look like if I planned and not reacted to it.

I was still unable to have dreams and aspirations at this point. I was so hard-wired to survive that I felt that dreams were dumb and a fantasy I could not afford to waste my time on. I had to focus on the things right in front of me that would get my immediate needs met- food, shelter, clothing, minimal happiness, safety, and security.

I enrolled back into school and started applying for jobs that paid more than minimum wage. After a few tries, I got a better paying job, working as a junior loan officer at a bank. With this job and the few part-time, low paying jobs (hostess, makeup artist, inventory taker, adult video store worker ,to name a few) and was able to move into an apartment with a girl I met at one of the places I worked. I did not have many friends, mainly just my roommate Sarah and we shared a love of dancing, red bull and sour gummy worms. I know, it was a friendship with such a rock-solid foundation, ha-ha. She was light-hearted and a good person. On the nights that we didn't work, we would practice these choreographed dance routines and go out to the clubs and dance. We were only nineteen and not old enough to go to bars and clubs, but Sarah was dating a guy who had a cousin who was a bouncer, so we were guaranteed access. We would go two and three times a week to dance and let loose. That meant that we saw this bouncer a lot.

One night Sarah mentioned to me that the bouncer had asked if I had a boyfriend and asked for my phone number. I spun around so fast I was dizzy and yelled "don't you dare give it him". I had no interest in guys or dating. I was afraid of men, both the physical aspects of being hurt, but I also feared that I would hurt them, or use them to not stand on my own two feet. I had watched my mother and grandmother manipulate men growing up and I didn't want to be anything like them. After hearing the bouncer might be interested in me, I lost my interest in going out to that bar and it was a struggle to sneak into other bars and clubs, so my dancing days came to an abrupt end.

Sarah was spending more and more time with her boyfriend and I was back to being a loner. I learned to enjoy my own company. I would go to the movies a lot. I loved the movies. I would go on walks and take myself out to eat occasionally when I could afford it.

One of these splurge meals brought me to Denny's restaurant. I was so poor that Denny's felt like an indulgence. After I ate, I was walking out of the restaurant feeling somewhat self-conscious because the waitress had been making comments to me about being a beautiful girl dining alone and other comments that made me feel weird.

I paid and nearly ran out of the restaurant, keeping my eyes on the ground to avoid eye contact with anyone that may be silently judging me for eating alone. I was so caught up in my thoughts that I failed to see the three people walking into the restaurant and I walked right into them. I looked up embarrassed and it was none other than the bouncer from the club. He was there with two women and I pushed past without a word. I heard him coming up behind me and calling out my name, but I ignored him, fumbling with my keys and rushing to my car. He came up and stood next to my car talking to me. I continued to get into my car and ignored him. He was persistent and I finally gave in and listened to what he was saying. He explained that he was there having dinner with his cousins and was wondering if I would want to get together after. I politely declined, so he asked if another time would be good. I really didn't want to, but I also didn't want to be rude, so I gave him my phone number.

He called and after some time talking and getting to know each other, we started spending a lot of time together. I recognized right away that he was unlike anyone I had ever dated or met. He was kind, hardworking, genuine and had goals and aspirations. I was excited that someone who was so good, would possibly like me let alone love me. I was so use to interacting with men who abused and hurt women that this was shockingly refreshing to learn there were men out there that didn't behave that way. We ended up in a serious relationship. One that I was ill-equipped for. I had no idea how to be a girlfriend, but I was exploring the idea of us being long-term friends. After some time, he proposed to me and while I did not see marriage as an option for me, I agreed.

He explained early on that he was unable to have children and I thought that was great- not for him, but for me. I did not want children. I had told him about my son, and he was very open and supportive. I learned that he had been married and was separated from his wife. She had a young son, and he was actively involved in the boy's life, which did not bother me at all. When he and I moved in together, I spent time with the boy and was happy to have the time to interact with a child who was around the age of my son, who I rarely got to see.

I had been going to school and was studying law. It was my goal to become a lawyer. I was intrigued by the justice system. Once I gained more knowledge, I helped my fiancé divorce his current wife.

I lived my life without deep emotions and often I could only express extreme anger. It was like I was numb or throttled back unless I was pushed to the emotional equivalent of a volcano erupting. Our relationship was a friendship with moments of potential to be something else, but truly I think we were just friends living together and trying to navigate life together. He was in college, there to play football and not really to learn. He had dreams of going into the military and I thought that was a great future for him. I had plans to continue in school and thought that he should continue with his plans to join the military.

He appreciated the support and enlisted in the Army. He had a delayed entry planned and was not leaving for a few months. I was busy in school with finals and preparing for my senior year of college. During finals week, I came down with what I thought was a bad flu and I went to the free health clinic near campus. I explained my symptoms and told them that I had the flu and needed something to help me get through finals week.

The nurse took some fluid samples and came back into the room moments later to tell me that I did not have the flu, but that I would be fine. I looked at her confused and said 'if it isn't the flu, what is it?" She smiled this huge smile and said "honey, you're pregnant" to which I promptly replied, "that's impossible, he can't have kids", through her choked laughter she said "oh, honey that's what they all say" and she left the room in a burst of hysterical laughter and said the doctor would be in shortly. I sat there in the silent and clinically stark room just stunned. How could this have happened and what was I going to do? I was a terrible mother and could not have more children. When the doctor came in, I was detached from the events that were taking place, I don't recall the conversation, but I walked out with a prescription for prenatal vitamins and a referral to an OBGYN.

I went home instead of going back to school, and my fiancé was sleeping after working all night as a security guard. I sat on the bed and said his name repeatedly until he awoke. Still half asleep, I shared with him that I was pregnant. He was overjoyed to say the least. He immediately started calling everyone he knew to tell them the good news, and within minutes his excessively large family was showing up and calling with congratulations and giving praise for God who delivered this miracle.

I adjusted my mask just enough to not bring down their happiness or offend them. I stayed in this state of disbelief for weeks. I continued attending school and a few short months later we were married, and weeks later he left for basic training. I struggled physically with the pregnancy, I was very sick and my inability to swallow properly, greatly impacted my baby. I

had only gained four pounds and was told that he was not growing as well as he should. I focused on nutrition and doing whatever I could to ensure this little baby would be born healthy. I
may be a proven crappy mom, but I would not let this child fail
to grow because of me, that was the part of motherhood that I
had previously gotten right. I shifted my focus from myself to
my child and that remained my focus. I grew to love this little
person growing inside of me, and when he was born 16 weeks
early, I was ready to be a mother. I had graduated from college
the week before he made his premature and dramatic entrance
into the world. 24 weeks of pregnancy changed me for the better. I was going to be the best mother and wife possible. I threw
myself into this new challenge of my life, completing abandoning my other plans.

I want to back up in the timeline for just a moment.
Something happened just before I became pregnant, and it
offers some insight to my state of mind and emotional state as
I ease into this life with my new fiancé. Earlier in my story, you
were briefly introduced to my grand-grandmother Noni. Noni
was my caretaker for much of my childhood, as I mentioned
and at that time, she and my Papa were already fairly advanced
in their years. As I grew, their age and failing health prevented
them from being there for me through the struggles I faced, and
my mother did not want me around them because they were

my dad's family and not hers. Noni was still my role model and I loved her more than I had ever loved anyone up until this point in my life. While I did not physically see her very often, I spoke to her on the phone and that connection and bond was the strongest one I had.

When I was twenty, my Noni passed away. This loss was tremendous for me. I felt like my anchor was cut and I was now drifting out to sea. My psychological safe haven was gone, and I was truly alone. I did not grow up in a religious family. When religion was spoken about, which was rare, there was a negative undertone to the conversation. I was told both indirectly and directly that organized religion was bad, and I don't recall there being much talk of God. My dad would sometimes speak of God, but it was in a context of him experiencing something when he was high. I did go to a few church services as a kid if I stayed over at someone's house on a Saturday night and their family attended church the next day, but I didn't connect these experiences to God or even to religion.

Church was a place we as children went to get treats and play. It was a laid-back environment and not a meaningful place. I also had that one experience with the Mormon church when I was marrying Jay and if you recall, I did not take that seriously either. I can safely say, I was Godless and had no understanding of anything related to God. God was not on my radar.

Noni was a well-loved member of the community she lived in, and was a local artist. Many people came to pay their respects to her at her funeral, which was held in a church that my grandmother, "the troubled one" arranged in what I think was an effort for us to look respectable as a family. At the funeral, the pastor asked if anyone in the family would like to speak. My family was distraught with grief and no one was a naturally gifted public speaker, so I felt comfortable hopping up on the platform to tell the room how wonderful my Noni was.

As I walked onto the stage, mic in hand, something came over me. It was the emotional volcano that filled the landscape inside me, and I couldn't stop it from erupting. Instead of telling the packed room about my wonderful Noni, I began to speak to God. I told him how much I hated him, how he just took the only thing that ever meant anything away from me and that there was nothing he would ever be able to do to replace this loss. I would have continued the lava flow of angry insults, but something came over me and I blacked out.

Some would say that I hyperventilated or passed out from grief, but they weren't in my body. I had passed out many times and there is always a warning. This was more like flipping a light switch, and something flipped my switch, and I was out. When I came to, I was freaked out. I was looking around the room to see if anyone else saw what had happened. I was so freaked out that I remained quiet for the rest of the day, and that was unlike me.

Another seed was planted. This seed would grow in the form of curiosity. When I would think about my light switch moment, I would grow both fearful and intrigued. I wanted to learn more, to see if God had the ability to do that, or was I just over dramatizing my grief. I didn't really know anyone who I felt would be a good source of information on God, so I turned to the only credible source for information that I knew, the library.

I went to the library and over a period of weeks I checked out and read every book about religion I could find. I read and absorbed as much information as I could. I was filled with knowledge but had no answers. I was confused, I should have understood by having read so much, but I didn't. I thought more and more on how I could figure this out. It dawned on me to call churches; duh, they would have all the answers about God. I pulled out the very thick phone book, turned to the section with churches and I began to call them in alphabetical order, one by one.

I must have called a hundred churches and with each call I became more and more disappointed. I would call them up when they answered, I would say "Hi, I'm Angela. Can you tell me about God and your church?" and nearly every reply was the same, "we would love to have you visit our church, we meet on Sundays at this time and this time; we hope you come". I had zero intentions of ever going to church. My family might not have taught me much good, but they taught me that organized religion was bad, they only wanted your money- to which I had none and the people who attended church were crazy. So nope, nope, nope- I was not going to open that pandora's box. But I was out of options, I was nearing the end of the churches in the phone book and I had no new answers or direction. I decided to call one more church.

It was about 6pm on a Friday night, I half expected no one would answer, so I was about to hang up after the third ring when a woman's voice said hello and thanked me for calling the church. I paused for a moment, the voice sounded older like it belonged to a sweet grandmotherly type, and I was exhausted from calling so many other churches, so I hurriedly and I suspect flippantly asked her the same question as all the other calls, and she responded "I would LOVE to" and for the next two hours she told me about the Episcopal church, the origin of the church, her background in the church and answered any question I was brave enough to ask. After two hours, she invited me to join her on Sunday for the church service at 9am and I agreed. All my doubt, fears and concerns were mitigated by her willingness to share her passion with me. I connected to her passion and not the subject matter.

I asked my fiancé to attend church with me that Sunday as I was truly scared to go alone and felt like I would chicken out. He agreed. I was nervous the rest of the evening and all of the next day. When Sunday came, we got up, got dressed and headed down to the car. I stopped at the mailbox and checked the mail as I passed by to the car. In the mailbox was a ticket that my fiancée got for speeding and not paying a bridge toll. The ticket was over $500. That was as much as our rent for a month. I was livid. I got into the car and as he pulled away heading to the church, I laid into him like never before. I continued to let the lava erupt from me and I was relentless and cruel with my words. He was so calm and patient with me, until he wasn't. About fifteen minutes into our drive, a few blocks from the church, he stopped the car in the middle of the road and told me to get out. He was tired of my shit, and tired of me yelling at him. I was so angry that I complied. I got out of the car and stomped off as he drove away. I was so angry that I could not think straight. I power-walked to the church, went right in, and sat down before I even could realize what I was doing.

As soon as I sat down and had a few minutes to collect my thoughts, I started to panic. I was in a church, in a full pew of strangers and I was all alone. I wanted to run but running would

GROWING THROUGH IT

first require me to climb over the legs of about eight strangers, so I sat still. The Episcopal services are very ritualistic and there are prompts given by Deacons and the crowd responds. I was not expecting this. Something would be said, and the entire congregation would respond in unison. I was freaked the hell out. I thought it was like mind-control or something.

I was near tears and desperately wanted to drop to the ground and crawl out unnoticed, but that was not an option, so I faked it the best I could. Just when I thought I could take it no more, everyone grew still and this priest in long, white robes proceeded down to the altar with young men surrounding him carrying things in the air that looked like flags and there was incense or something burning from an urn-like pot. I was slightly mesmerized.

When he got to the podium, he began to speak, and his voice was so deep and clear. At first, I couldn't even focus on his words, as his voice was just so smooth, like the voice you would hear coming from a radio host. When I tuned into his words, I realized he was talking about something called All Saints Day and apparently it was that day, and he went into telling a story of a green-eyed, redheaded little girl that was so desperately lost. You guys, I was redheaded and green eyed, and I too was lost. My body had chills. The entire story felt like it was or could be about me. Now, I was really scared.

93

As soon as the service was over, I bolted for the door. I was not even attempting a graceful exit; it was all elbows and very few pardon me's. Just as I reached the door, I heard the voice of the woman from the phone. She called me by name, came up to me, looped her arm through mine and told me that she was so glad I came and steered me towards something called the fellowship hall where we were going to have cookies. That day, I began my walk with Christ. One year to the day of my Noni's death is when my son was born, 16 weeks premature. I challenged God and he showed me. That little baby would soften my heart and continue me on a path that I am so grateful for today.

Having this new little baby and being a part of a church community for the first time in my life, I began to feel less alone. I attended church every week. I signed up for confirmation classes and I was doing my best to pack in years of missed spiritual enrichment into my mind. I would often get embarrassed or frustrated. When someone would reference a Bible story, and I would stare blankly back at them, they would say something to the effect of "you know, Moses?, or "you know the story of Jacob that you heard when you were a child?". Umm, no, I did not know Moses, Jacob, or anyone else that they were referring to and I, as a now full-grown adult felt stupid for not having the ability to reference a childhood that included these "basic" knowledge points. While it was never their intention to shame me, they genuinely could not grasp that a person my age had NEVER heard of these stories. In response to my shame and embarrassment, I stopped asking meaningful questions and I withdrew myself enough to protect myself. I would still attend church, I would complete the confirmation class, I would along with my baby be baptized, but I was disconnected in the most important way.

My heart had been hardened to this Christian community. Not hardened by hate, but rather it was hardened by a lack of connection. As soon as we moved from the area to continue in my husband's military career, I did not stay in contact and I would not seek out a new church to join. There would be times over the years that I would feel that yearning for community, for a closer relationship with Jesus, for that love and connection, but I was unwilling to be uncomfortable.

I was processing a lot all at once during this timeframe, I was recently married, a new mom again, a recent college graduate, the recent loss of my Noni and facing a move from California to Louisiana in response to orders my new husband received from the Army.

I was feeling pretty raw at this point. My biological family, dad, grandmother, and uncles were all coming together to sift through my Noni's house and like I have read about typical families, they would fight and squabble over this item or that item. I didn't want anything. Stuff was just that to me, it was stuff. I knew that things would not fill my void. While we were all gathered, I did take my first step in attempting to really process and heal from the sexual abuse I suffered. Not knowing how to discuss it, or bring it up, I used my limited emotional vocabulary, coupled with my hardened heart, and while we were all sitting around one day, I said "remember when Walt used to molest me".

Looking back, this was likely not the best way to process my pain and memories with my uncles and father. I recall their faces; they were pale, and their eyes were a mix of sadness and panic. No one wanted to make eye contact with me, and no one wanted to engage in the conversation. While I didn't really receive a response, I also wasn't looking for one. I wanted to be heard. I wanted my secret to surface just enough to be freeing. We never have spoken about the abuse, not on that sad day as we said goodbye to our childhood memories and all the tangible items attached to our life together and not now as adults.

I am not angry or upset at their silence, those useless emotions left my heart long ago. I feel bad for them, that they didn't know how to comfort me through my pain or the loss of my innocence. I am more saddened that as a society, we are not able to sit with victims in their grief and pain and support them through it.

Bad things happen to all of us, but so often, we are expected to swallow those experiences and not let them negatively affect others. So these powerful emotions, they sit deep inside us, often festering and growing until we are no longer ourselves. We are unable to connect to others in the same way we would have if we had not experienced trauma, or if we had been supported through the growing process needed to overcome the trauma. What if we altered that part of our culture? What if we took down our masks, grieved together, hurt together, and healed together? I suspect if we normalized trauma, not in a "it's ok to hurt people" kind of way, but in a "we all have things that have hurt us" kind of way, we would live in a more pleasant society. For me personally, I also strongly see the link between mental illness, depression, and anxiety and those who have experienced trauma. Unresolved trauma, neglect and abuse affects us all, even if you have not directly been a victim. It is shaping the world you live in.

Chapter Five

THE BASIC YEARS OF GETTING IT WRONG

The next decade of my life while trauma free, would not equate to a happy life or a fulfilled life. I was going through the motions and navigating the best I could. I was realizing very quickly that I was ill-equipped to live a domestic life. I had no idea how to be a mother, a wife, a housekeeper, a bill payer, a friend, or even a woman. I also didn't feel that I had anyone to turn to teach me these basic life skills. I had no relationship with my mother or her family, my grandmother had to be cut out of my life due to her earlier behavior and treatment of me, my dad was busy trying to stay clean and figure out his life, and my siblings were little kids. I had moved away from California which is the only place and people I had ever known. In the beginning of this decade, I was living in a rural part of Louisiana on a military base. I instantly fell in love with the close culture of the military lifestyle. People seemed to band together and I was introduced to structured lifestyles for the first time. I fell in love with the routine of my life. Each day was a lot like the day prior and through this pattern of repetitiveness, I was able to find comfort in knowing what to expect. I was even starting to make a few friends, other Army wives who lived near me and had children the same age as my son. I would say that beyond having spouses in the same line of work and children around the same ages, we did not have much else in common or at least the conversations stayed at the surface level for the most part.

I learned to enjoy living life at the surface level. I felt my "mask" taking shape. I was a young woman who was from California, married with one son, educated, pretty and kind. This was what I would show people. Surface-level living was tough. My husband and I did not have an amazing marriage to say the least. We were friends who should not have gotten married or started a family. We struggled to navigate married life together. I would try to lean on him to help me learn the ins and outs of my new role in life and he was busy focusing on his military career. I was growing more and more lonely, as the surface-level friendships were doing very little for my soul and they were more about passing time, and less about experiencing connection.

Motherhood without someone to really learn from or

talk to about my experience and struggles was tough too. I now know that much of what I was feeling was normal, even if at the time I felt isolated and abnormal. I would be lucky if I got a shower in a few times a week, and I was exhausted trying to keep up on the house and raise an infant by myself. I had never been great at self-care, housework, or life, but the motherhood obstacle seemed to magnify and expose my weaknesses. I needed help, I needed attention and I was alone.

One desperate afternoon, my husband would return home from work, he likely had worked a ten-hour day and I had been eagerly pacing the living room waiting for him to come home and give me a break. He walked in the door and I rushed over to him, baby in hand and said "here, your turn". He responded that he couldn't help me because he hurt his shoulder. What! I NEED the help is all I could think, take your baby! He did seem to have an injury, so my face and mood softened some and I asked him in my most caring, newly acquired, nice wife voice, what had happened? He responded that his First Sergeant had him and a few other soldiers wrestling at lunch and while he was able to take every guy, they put in front of him, he hurt his shoulder in the process. Now, I don't want you to get the wrong impression of me, but I can be a lot of hot lava spewing, fire-breathing balls of anger at times and my response to my husband was unkind. I was livid that he had spent any part of his day wrestling with other men for the enjoyment of his superiors while I was home, un-showered, exhausted, and lonely. Before he could stop me, I was on the phone with his First Sergeant giving him a piece of my mind about his shitty-ass leadership and how it was affecting me. I read that man the riot act and cursed him up one side and down another. I am sure he was not expecting that type of call from a Private's wife. I had no sense in my head it would seem to anyone around me, including my husband.

Honestly, I had no context on how the military really worked or the chain of command, or the respect that went with that. I also didn't care in that moment of desperation. My husband likely didn't sleep a wink that night in fear of what would be waiting for him at work the next day. He was a good soldier and got up and went to work to face the music. Later that next day, my husband returned home with his First Sergeant. This man was gigantic, he towered over me at a minimum of six foot six and was a solid rock of muscle, I am guessing nearing 300lbs and he threw around his size in a clear effort to intimidate people to get his way. He had come to my house with the intention of putting me in my place, and letting me know what was expected of me as a respectable Army wife.

The conversation did not go his way. He may have been tall and large, but I was a mouthy force to be reckoned with. I enjoyed matching wits with this man and not backing down to his tactics. He left that day with what I think was a healthy respect for my opinion and I for his. A few weeks later they left on short notice for a twelve-month deployment to Iraq.

While other spouses were sad and concerned, I was numb. I was back to survival mode, trying to figure out how to navigate this new set of challenges. Many of my surface-level friends were returning to their hometowns which meant the base was relatively empty and I was unsettled.

My newfound love of routine was gone, and I was lost. I started experiencing a lot of anxiety and I felt depressed. To cope with my feelings, I started looking for work. While there were not a lot of opportunities in this small community, I knew there had to be some. At that time, the Army was launching some new community enrichment programs and my degree was in Human Services Management and Business Administration which was exactly what they were looking for. I was fantastic at interviewing, because they involve surface level, technical conversations and no real emotion or depth is needed, so I nailed it.

I was hired by the Community Services Office. I would be working with a woman who was dynamic and passionate. Among other social services and legal skills, she was an entomologist who worked as a coroner with law enforcement ,on cases to determine cause of death and timeline. She was contracted to work on a prevention program related to domestic violence. We connected right away, and I opened up and shared with her about my abuse background as a survivor. She was amazed by my strength and journey and with her guidance, I began to speak nationally on domestic violence survivor panels along with working alongside her to develop curriculum which would be used to prevent domestic violence in military families and to help victims.

I really enjoyed this work. I felt that I had purpose and was helping people for the first time in my life, I was driven by something other than survival. I also felt that I had found something I was good at and my confidence in being an adult was growing. I continued focusing on this work, the entire deployment and when the deployment was extended another 12 months, I was fine with this. I could stay doing what I loved to do.

During that time, I was in a bad car accident and my esophagus was reinjured. This caused my eating and nutritional difficulties to increase. I returned to California for a brief time to get help with my son while I underwent surgeries to repair the new damage. My former church family graciously opened their arms to me and my son, providing us with a place to stay and support with childcare while I received medical care and recovered.

When I returned to Louisiana, I didn't have a car and that First Sergeant that I had interacted with in such a passionate and negative way, offered to give me his car to use since he was still deployed with my husband, and would not be using it. These two acts of true and monumental kindness changed my perspective on people, just slightly. I began to see that there was goodness in the world that was not based on relationships, guilt, or obligation, but that there was a level of kindness that just existed to exist.

Being back in Louisiana was tough, the funding for the program that I was working on was cut and I was laid off, my surface-level friends were still gone, my marriage was rapidly deteriorating. The extended absence from the deployment was showing both of us that our connection was more platonic than anything else and neither of us felt we wanted to make a marriage work. Friendship, sure but not marriage. So once again I was lost.

I started hanging out with a new crowd that closely resembled my old, old crowd from my childhood and I began to make poor decisions. I was back to survival mode and the growth that I had experienced seemed to have been lost completely. I welcomed back my bad habits like an old friend, and I escaped into this darkness for some time. My husband returned from his two-year long deployment and we were fighting constantly.

We had almost no connection, no desire for a future together and we both felt stuck. The Army anticipated that the extended absences would have a negative impact on marriages and families, so they blanketed us with support. It was generic, one-size-fits-all support, and while we continued to try for the sake of our children, we both knew in our hearts that it wasn't going to work. In a last-ditch effort to reconcile our family, we took an extended trip throughout the South and spent a considerable amount of time at Disneyworld. While it was a nice enough vacation to end our active fighting, it was not enough to ultimately save our marriage. When we returned home from vacation, we had received a new set of military orders and we were temporarily distracted by the upcoming move.

The thing with military life is you get to experience a lot of life, see a lot of places and it's generally an enjoyable life, but it doesn't allow you to create roots or strong attachments for the most part. At times, I think I had learned to love the unpredictability military life provided, it wasn't me that was unstable and struggling, it was this lifestyle making it difficult for me to create lasting relationships and a foundation. I could hide behind the lifestyle and my mask.

Our next duty station would take us to New York. Life was better in New York, I was able to find work right away working on another meaningful community services project for the Army, this time helping children and families affected by the war and the extended and frequent deployments. I made a few deeper friendships as well and I made a few friends who I trusted enough to share a little bit about my story, not much, but it was a huge step for me. My marriage was mainly a roommate/friendship relationship at this time, and we would often speak about divorcing. We weren't happy but we weren't sure what to do about it. While I wasn't attending church and had not attended church for years, I felt a strong pull to go to school to become a pastor. My husband at the time was supportive but really disconnected from what I was doing, so I went back to school, but I didn't pursue a career in ministry. I felt unqualified. I had a desire but felt unworthy. I also enjoyed the new layers of the "mask" I was used to wearing and I didn't want to risk letting anyone in too far.

On my current career path, I was travelling to many states and was serving thousands of military families, I was working with Congress, lawmakers, was a guest speaker on local TV shows and was working passionately to help others. I was using all of this as a distraction from dealing with my issues with motherhood, my failing marriage, my lack of self-identity and my inability to create close relationships. I had perfected my public "mask" as a do gooder and workaholic. I would work around the clock and when I wasn't working, I was pursuing my education. I managed to raise my son, the younger of the two who lived with me, but it was not the quality of life he deserved. I was emotionally absent, constantly stressed, depressed and anxious when I was not focused on work, a project or school.

Anytime I needed to feel real feelings, I would only be able to express anger, hostility, and other negative emotions. That doesn't mean I didn't love my son, I loved him tremendously and protected him profusely from the world, but I was unable to express love in a soft, gentle and motherly way. I went through the motions of motherhood carefully trying not to feel anything and not to make any missteps that would harm my child. I had no idea that in the process of building a better life for us, and surviving life, I would not be giving him the time and attention he needed to flourish.

I don't have many regrets in my life, but this is one of them. My son was such a wonderful child, so loving and sweet and I wish I would have been capable at the time to slow down and just love him. To be able to experience his childhood with him instead of racing through it just trying to survive. Most of the time we were stationed in New York, my husband was deployed, rarely coming home on leave which further divided us and we continued to grow further apart. During one of his leave visits, I got pregnant with my daughter. We were not in love, but I think both of us were grasping at straws. We wanted something that seemed to be unobtainable.

During my pregnancy, I learned that my daughter would be born with a single kidney and would likely have some health challenges. I could barely parent the child I was raising, how was I going to parent a special needs child? Like most things I faced, I just powered through it trying to feel as little as possible. I continued to work and was finishing up school during my pregnancy. The deployment was causing even more strain on our marriage and I wanted to return to the area of the country that I knew. I had nowhere to go and very few people who I felt would receive me. Again, I was lost.

I began to petition the Army to move me back to California. At this point, as my pregnancy continued and the fate of my child's health was unclear, I was feeling desperate enough to even return to my biological family if I had no other option. Just prior to my daughter's birth, the Army agreed to send us to Washington State as there were no California bases needing my husband's MOS at that time. Just after my daughter was born, I loaded up the kids and drove to our new home in Washington.

At this point, I knew my marriage was over and I was feeling that Washington would offer me and the kids a fresh start. I had some familiarity with Southern Washington, as a child when I would occasionally visit my maternal grandmother. The landscape of Seattle felt a lot like the Bay Area which was the home I had known as a child and young adult. I settled in quickly and was able to find a job right away. This time, I was working for military housing which I had done briefly in New York when the funding for the social service project had run out. My daughter was doing well despite the original prognosis. Life felt ok. Knowing that my marriage was ending, I was able to begin to see myself as a long-term resident of Washington and I purchased a home South of Seattle. I quickly made friends, connected with some old friends who had moved to Seattle from California and I was less lost than I had ever been. I officially separated from my husband who was deployed again, and I settled into making a life as a single mother.

Chapter Six

THE LOVE I WASN'T READY FOR

I n Washington, life pulled together so quickly. I had a friends' group, a good job, a home, and all within months of arriving.

I had an old childhood friend move into my house with me along with his children. We would trade off childcare. This allowed me to expand my social life and get out with my friends. I absolutely loved to dance. I would go to bars and clubs as often as possible to just dance. My girlfriends were also huge fans of going out, and they loved going with me since I didn't drink. I had given up drinking and partying the year I turned nineteen and had no desire to complicate my life by tempting myself with addiction problems. I had learned by watching my parents and those around me, the impact drugs and alcohol could have on a life and I was struggling without those barriers, so I couldn't risk adding anything to my growing list of things I survived. While I was willing to be the designated driver, I hated driving, so I always wanted to stay close to home.

There was a little bar a mile from my house and that is where we would go a few nights a week. The music was good, the crowd was mild, and I was mostly unbothered by men there. I could go and have a good time and go home alone. While I was open to the idea of one day having a relationship, I was going to try and avoid it for as long as possible. Now, I wasn't a nun, more of a wounded bird, so I would dance with guys sometimes and when they asked for my number or to see me again, I would give them a fake number and move on. It was rare for me to show interest in anyone.

There was a guy who I would see at the bar often and I assume he was a local, because I would see him at the gas station and the grocery store, etc. There was a pull that I felt whenever I saw him, but I was careful not to make eye contact or engage in a conversation with him. I didn't trust that feeling I had.

There was only one other person in my history that I felt that pull towards and that guy nearly killed me-literally. I would learn my lesson and admire this man from a distance, and I did for weeks. I began to see him more and more, it was weird. He seemed to be a lot of places I visited, but I was never tempted to speak to him. I was afraid of what might happen if I did.

A few more weeks passed by and it was Halloween. Halloween is my favorite time of year and I love dressing up in costume. I already wore a mask each day, but during Halloween I could do so openly. My friends and I decided we would dress up and head out to a party, an hour from home. I wasn't thrilled with the idea of driving so far from home, but my one friend was really into a firefighter she met, and she begged me to drive them, so we went. The party was lame, there was no dancing, only lots of drinking and chatting. I hated small talk and didn't drink so I wanted to leave.

It took some convincing, but my friends agreed to go to the bar we attended regularly by my house, so we ended up there. It was packed that night and the atmosphere was so fun. We were dancing and laughing and having the best time. I noticed that guy that I felt the pull towards was there and he was dancing which I did not recall seeing him do normally. He was more of a sideline, drinking, kind of guy from my observations. He was dancing with this girl, super close and he was putting his hat on her head. I am not sure what came over me, but I walked up to them, pushed her out of the way and started dancing with him. While I was once a wild and rambuctiousgirl, the years had mellowed me out some, but I guess that firecracker within me was not dead, just dormant. My friends, who never expected this behavior from me, looked on from the sidelines in awe and were half expecting there to be a fight. There wasn't a fight.

He and I danced the rest of the evening together. At the

end of the night, he asked me for my number, and I gave it to him, my real number. My friends gave me a hard time as my behavior seemed almost supernatural to them. It did to me too. He called the next day, and we went on a date the following night and nearly fifteen years later we are still together.

I would love to say that it has been a blissful fifteen years, but it hasn't been. When I gave him my number, I knew in my heart that I was not ready for a meaningful relationship. I was unwilling to work on myself and fully heal from my trauma. Now, these were not conscious thoughts but, in my heart, I knew I was a mess and I felt unlovable. Luckily, this man was strong, loyal, patient, and willing to push through the disasters that I often would create. I may seem harsh on myself, taking the blame for much of what happened, but I am now healed and mature enough to look back and recognize with certainty that I had a habit of self-destructing. I didn't know better for many years, and he wasn't prepared for what his heart signed him up for.

Zack and I moved in together basically the week that we officially met. I was a mother of three who was separated from my husband. He was a kid who was barely out of high school and had just ended his first real relationship with the girl he dated all through high school. I had lived this big, tumultuous life, and was full of life experience and he was relatively new to adulthood. We could not have been more mismatched on the surface, but underneath the surface we would be a force in the making. I was far into my career at this point, not that I intentionally had planned a career. Zack was working but not focused on a career. We were both just living life, seeing where it would take us.

Within a few months of meeting, I was offered a job in Oregon which would require me to relocate to Portland. Zack didn't hesitate, he was coming with me. He quit his job and was a stay-at-home dad to my two children. It would take me years to appreciate the sacrifice that this was. He had no idea how to be a dad, or a step-parent. His younger brother was the same age as my middle child who, was three years old, and my daughter was a baby. This was unfamiliar territory for us all.

Like most things in my life, I gave it little thought and was just focused on surviving and taking care of my family. Zack and I were really connected. I was deeply in love. I loved Zack in the same way I had loved Jay, it was an all-in type of love. I was one hundred percent committed to him and could never imagine having eyes for anyone else. You would think that a love that strong would be enough to know how to behave, how to be married, how to fulfill your partner, but nope it wasn't.

Having never had real role models in these areas and no one in my life was married or happily married, I was at a loss on what I was doing or how I was doing it. Zack lacked life experience and I severely lacked emotional maturity. This combination caused us a lot of hurt over the years. I inflicted emotional pain on him unintentionally. I just had no idea how to be connected to someone. My love for him and my children was so strong that I was committed to figuring it out.

For the first time in my life, I was willing to open up the scars and deep-rooted hurt and heal them. I chose to be in a growth mindset and would actively avoid causing others pain. These may be baseline behaviors for you, but for me, these were revolutionary concepts. I would fail more often than I would succeed. I would have seasons where I would just give up and focus on being a workaholic, feeling that the best way I could love my family was to provide for them. I have discovered over the years that for me to be the best version of myself, I would have to choose to fight my battles daily. I would half-ass it, doing just the bare minimum, or read a self-help book and not put anything into practice. It was going to take all my effort to win this war within me. I was finally able to articulate what I wanted but now, I needed to put the work in.

Putting the work in, as it relates to improving myself, is where I have a history of falling short. My head will be full of knowledge, my heart will be in the right place and yet I am still frozen in inaction. To overcome this, I had to dive deeper. When do I freeze? What seems to be my trigger? To figure this out, I observed myself over a period of a week, each time my mind and my actions were in paradox, I would write it down. An example of this would be me telling myself on my drive home that I will go for a run when I got home, but then I pull into my driveway, go inside and sit on the couch and scroll through Facebook until my kids would interrupt me and ask me what was for dinner. That went on my list.

What my observations revealed to me over the week, was this scenario played out again and again in different contexts. I would make a commitment to myself; I would look forward to the commitment, I would choose a mindless task like scrolling through the internet or watching TV instead of following through on my commitment. What I also observed was that when someone outside of myself needed something of me, I was quick to jump to care for their needs. This came in different forms: my dog needed to be walked twice a day; my children needed to eat or help with their schoolwork; my husband needed a hand with a project; or a friend needed me to listen and give advice. It didn't matter what the need was, when I was needed, I jumped into action. I would prioritize fulfilling their needs, but I would hide from my own needs.

The reason, the "why" behind my pattern was much harder to identify and I had to do some mining deep within me to figure out what was driving my behavior. What I learned was something so simple, my pattern was driven by instant gratification.

When I worked on myself whether that was mental, physical, or spiritual work, the progress is more gradual, and the results take time. While I would wait for the results, I would get discouraged and distracted. Conversely, when I helped someone else, they immediately expressed their gratitude, and their thankfulness would pump me up. I became addicted to the feeling that I received when I was pleasing people. I hate the term "people pleaser". It always held such a negative connotation and would often be used to describe a person who I felt had very little self-worth and value. Those were weak qualities, and I never wanted to be described as weak. The dictionary defines a people pleaser as "someone who tries hard to make others happy. They go out of their way to please someone, even if it means taking their own valuable time or resources away from themselves". Ugh, that is what I do. It is me; I am a dreaded people pleaser. I know that this stems from my upbringing and wanting connection with others and relationships. In my damaged mind, love is earned and not freely given. While I know that this is not true of many, it is what I extracted from my interactions with others while growing up.

Knowing these things about myself, the patterns I use

to self-sabotage and the reasons for my actions, I am better equipped to manage my own toxic behaviors. While helping people is a great quality and it is what I love to do in my life, I had to classify it as a toxic trait, when I was doing it as a way to distract me from working on myself and achieving my own goals and needs.

The strategy that has worked for me, to balance my need to please people with my need to take care of myself is:

- **Make Commitments:** At the end of each day, I take time to reflect on the day and make commitments to myself for the next day. If I spend too much time on my phone, or watching tv, I made a new commitment for the next day to limit TV to this time or that time and I plan my day in a way that does not allow me idle time to distract myself.

- **Choose a Weekly Focus:** I choose one thing a week to focus on. That may be healthy eating in the form of meal planning or setting a timer to remind me to eat throughout the day, or trying a plant-based recipe, skipping the drive through when going to and from work, going to bed early to get in the right amount of sleep I need, or scheduling time to exercise by myself or with a friend. Adding or eliminating one thing a week has helped me to build healthier habits and take care of myself.

- **Schedule Time to Help:** I stopped saying yes to every opportunity there was to help someone. If the need was not immediate, I ask if I can schedule a time to help and suggest a time that works around the commitments, I have made for myself.

- **Prioritize Self Care Rituals:** I fell in love with taking care of myself. I bought myself great smelling lotion that made me excited to soak in a bath and then lather myself with this feel-good scent. I learned to love the way my skin felt after taking my make-up off for the day, so much so that I look forward to this routine each night. I bought myself a bright colored toothbrush that makes me feel fun and whimsical when I brush my teeth.

Having the love of someone else made it possible for me to begin to heal from the hurts created within me by others. Ultimately, the love I needed was the love of self, and without that piece I would struggle to truly love anyone else. I learned that I deserve a give and take relationship with myself.

To really please the people around me, to create meaningful

relationships and to be a good friend, wife, mother, coworker, leader, I needed to take the time to prioritize myself and my needs, to then be able to give of myself when the opportunities arose.

Chapter Seven

HARD WORK PAYS OFF

I was approaching thirty when I had that epiphany: I was standing in my own way and it was me who I needed to change and not those around me. How I was raised, the trauma I experienced, and the hardships I survived could no longer be the reason I wasn't thriving. I began to read self- help books and I sought out a counselor. I had stopped counseling when instead of it being a coddling session focused on how I was mistreated, it shifted to me being responsible for my own future. I regret that. I was unwilling to let that truth sink into me at nineteen, at least not fully. It was a planted seed, but I failed to water it.

I think part of me was afraid to lose the labels that others put on me, to define me. Being a "601 kid" was why teachers and school officials supported me, not true, but in my imma- ture brain that was the link. Being a domestic violence sur- vivor defined me as being strong and capable of getting through the hard times in life. Surviving homelessness both as a kid and a young adult, proved I could take care of myself. Becoming a legal adult as a child showed my intelligence. All of these labels became my identity, instead of things that happened to me. I associated myself with trauma, I identified as a strong person when I had to overcome something. Essentially, my self-pro-claimed identity struggled to exist in "normal" conditions.

I would feel like an imposter or like I was wearing a mask when I was not faced with adversity or trauma. I thought that growth could only sprout from hurt, tragedy, pain, and dark-ness. Now, I had no conscious acknowledgement of this. I would not intentionally look for trouble or make trouble for myself, but I was my best self when I was rising to the occasion ,what-ever that was. and the harder the better.

My comfort zone was one messed up place and that is the place I would gravitate towards without even knowing it. Even something as simple as having an orderly house was diffi-cult for me because chaos was what was comfortable. I think if I had consistently gone to counseling, gone to a therapist trained to help childhood trauma survivors, opened up while in coun-seling or revealed my true self, I could have gotten help figuring this out. I took the hard route of trying to self-diagnose and heal alone and it was a slow journey.

For years, I gave up on friendships because I felt something was wrong with me and I could not articulate what it was or what I was healing from. I didn't know how to sit with someone in their feelings. I would either sit there obviously uncomfortable or I would offer advice and try to tell them how to fix their issues.

I tried to push my loyal and loving husband away rather than admit I was weak, scared and hurting. I also would rise to fight if I saw one on the horizon rather than trying to partner and working at keeping the peace. I had it so ingrained in me that any man having authority over me was a recipe for disaster that I refused to listen to him even when he had good ideas or advice.

The fear of being vulnerable has driven me to push so many people away. I also struggled to talk about myself, I would avoid that trap at nearly all costs. I am not even talking about big things; I would avoid any level of small talk because I did not want to reveal even the simplest thing about myself. I was a great listener, a good interviewer, a great host but anything that required a glimpse of vulnerability had me running scared. I had such a mistrust of people when it came to my emotions and thoughts. I was kind, would do anything for anyone, unless it involved giving of myself. I had learned to overcome by pleasing people, but I had no idea how to create and foster relationships.

All this self-work or as I would sometimes feel like, it was self-torture, it began to pay off. I had started off reading self-help books more geared towards professional development. I was very comfortable at work if the focus was on my performance, technical skills and the like and not on interpersonal relationships. These books helped me hone my skills and talents and improve in the workplace. My career was excelling. I was being given progressive responsibilities, promotions and significant salary increases. I learned that I was good at managing a lot at once, developing people and achieving results. In a short timeframe, I was promoted to President of my company, becoming the first woman and the youngest Company President in their thirty-year history.

This growth in my career was huge for my identity. It proved to me that with hard work, I could achieve whatever I desired. My dad was correct, I could become whatever I wanted to me. I leveraged my strength and grit to propel my career. I had a life that many would envy from the outside in. I was successful but I was profoundly unhappy.

Managing a team of people, mentoring people 1:1 is not the same as building relationships. This was more of me, giving of myself, and keeping up those walls to protect my vulnerabilities. What I wanted was personal relationships and personal connections; what I was creating was business relationships.

This confusion left me successful, but lonely and unfulfilled. My success only isolated me further as it required me to maintain a level of professionalism that fortified the mask, I was already wearing to shield my true self, my damaged self, my vulnerable self.

I learned that the skills that make you a good leader and a good business person are not the same that makes you a good wife, mother, and friend. How could I be so great in one area and be failing so miserably in the area my heart most desired? The answer was, for me, the foundation of how to be relational with others on a personal level was missing. Parents are our primary attachment figures, and they play a vital role in how we experience the world. In practice, our parents lay the foundation and shape what the world is going to be like for us. I had no role models for this, there was no school or college to attend to help me learn it and I was too wounded to continue a trial-and-error approach.

I think it is worth noting that not all childhood trauma survivors will experience the same outcomes as adults. While it is likely that an adult survivor will experience emotional, physical, or behavioral symptoms, not all will react in the same way, for the same duration, or at the same frequency. Our brains are all wired differently, and the impact of trauma is unique to the individual. Knowing that it is possible, and what the symptoms are, can help you identify in yourself or in someone else opportunities to provide resources and support.

From my research, I gathered that children are products of their own environments, and as adults we will often repeat the same behaviors we witnessed as a child. This was horrifying to me, that could not be how my life would go. I could not allow my experience of childhood trauma to continue to compromise my ability to form and maintain healthy bonds going forward. I was going to use my self-awareness and my love of learning to break the cycle. This was not an easy feat to take on, and I want to be upfront in saying that I am not healed; I am a work in progress. Here are some tangible steps that I took that may help you as well:

- **Educate Yourself**: Read books about healing from trauma, recovering from trauma, treatment for trauma. Attend seminars or discussions. Education is a tool; it allows us to be armed and equipped with information that can help us both now and later.

- **Find Support**: This may be a trusted friend, a therapist, your partner, or another survivor who has worked through their trauma. Having someone who will listen to you and love you through your growth and challenges is vital to recovery.

- **Cognitive Behavioral Therapy**: If you are looking for

a therapist, find one that specializes in adult recovery from childhood trauma. I found those that specialize in Cognitive Behavioral Therapy, which is trauma-focused psychotherapy, that helps patients change destructive patterns such as negative emotional, behavioral, and thought patterns into positive solutions through the use of awareness and cognitive responses, provide the most impact. I personally did not enjoy counseling when it involved the therapist passively listening to me; what I needed was action steps to help me learn to move forward in an improved way. This type of therapy was just that; practical directives to apply to my everyday life.

- **Faith and Spirituality:** My faith has been paramount in my healing journey. The faith community that I have surrounded myself with, have been so in tune with my needs as a survivor and they choose to love me through my growth journey. If you are not a person who has a relationship with God, I encourage you to seek Him out. If you have a relationship with Him but would like it to grow deeper, I encourage you to read your bible and seek out a faith community. I craved human connection, but I truly needed God in my life to surrender my pain to and begin to heal.

I am thankful that I chose to find a path to healing early enough in life to where I am positioned to enjoy a healthier "second half". I have an opportunity to see the benefits of my hard work be realized in my children and my future grandchildren. The cycle of abuse, trauma and neglect ends with me. This is a battle I wake up, willing to fight each day. It is a series of hard work that I am dedicating my life to, not only to benefit me personally but to show other survivors that it is possible. We get to choose; we get to decide if our scars are victory stripes or crippling reminders of our past.

Chapter Eight

NOW THIS IS MOTHERHOOD

I think for most of my time as a mother, which has been over half of my life, I resigned that I was just not cut out for motherhood. I was a good provider, but not a good nurturer. I had always been supportive of my children, but I struggled to show affection and love. I would often get caught up in my own troubles and worries or needs and this made me seem cold, distracted, stressed, and at times mean. I didn't know what I didn't know. In this regard, I was a product of my environment. I had not been shown affection as a child or appropriate love, so I was not only unable to understand how to parent in this way, but I also didn't even realize for years that this was a problem.

My motherhood focus was rather narrow; I wanted to protect my children and provide for them. I wanted to do for them what had not been done for me. This was such a one-dimensional view of how to raise a child. I didn't realize that there was so much more to it. My children needed guidance, affection, conversation, attention and most importantly time. I am embarrassed to say that I did not understand these other dimensions of parenthood, for many years and many children later.

If you ask my children, they will say that they were loved and provided for and kept safe, but that they did not have that deep connection with their mother that they yearned for. I too was shorting myself and I didn't even know it. The balance of what they needed and what I needed was a struggle. I so desperately wanted to provide them a life outside of the abuse and poverty I experienced, that I was blind to the importance of having an emotional bond with them.

I went on like this for twenty-five years of motherhood. For twenty-five years I was letting life just fly by, one act of survival after another. I would liken my approach to parenting to be more animal-like than human. In animal groups where offspring are born underdeveloped and lacking independence at birth, the parental animal provides nutrition, and teaches their offspring basic survival skills. Since parental care is costly and often affects the parent's own future survival, parental animals will make sure that any investment made into their offspring is well-spent. I can relate to that approach. I wanted the very best for my children, but my thought process was extremely superficial and immature.

I choose not to dwell on my inferior parenting abilities for all those years, but like most things in my life, I look at them as a learning opportunity. I never understood the saying "when you know better, you do better". This saying seemed so silly to me and inconsequential, but it is so true. I would like to say that I just woke up one day and realized that I needed to be a better mother, but it wasn't that easy. Pain is life's greatest teacher. It was a slow evolution of awareness, as my children grew older, and less dependent on me, I realized that I heard and saw from them less and less. Initially, my sensible brain related this to independence, and I wrote it off and moved on. Well, mostly I moved on. There was a small part of me, a growing emotional intellect, that warned me that this was an area of my life that I needed to look deeper into. The ironic part of all of this is that in a professional setting, I was known for my emotional intelligence and providing support and understanding in spades, to my team members and those I supervised and mentored. How could I be so in tune with the emotional needs of others, who were essentially strangers to me in the big picture and not recognize the true needs of my own household? The answer to that is poignant, the bible says, "For where your treasure is, there will your heart be also". I had poured nearly all of myself into my work, I was so focused on having a successful career, so I could support my family's needs, that I was blind to the other areas of my life. When Covid hit and the world dramatically began to change, my focus changed as well. The hours I had been spending away from my house were immediately halted. The adapting work world needed me less and less it seemed. Working remotely made employees more independent and effective. My ninety-hour work week nearly instantly was cut in half. At the same time, my husband was experiencing something similar with his role and my two children, who still lived at home, were home. The four of us, our family, began to experience undistracted life together for the first time.

It took some weeks of Zack, and I being home consistently and not being attached to our laptops and cellphones for the kids to decide it was beneficial for them to spend less time in their rooms and more time in the communal areas of our home. It was beautiful, like the slow bloom of a rose. As our life and relationships began to deepen, my heart began to shift. I went from waking up in the morning and immediately grabbing my phone or computer and answering emails, or working on spreadsheets, to excitedly waiting for my children to wake up and have breakfast with me, or take a family walk around the neighborhood.

There was a greater focus on family time from everyone in the house. The kids began to ask us for help with their homework, advice on friendships, and just everyday conversations were occurring. This may be a regular occurrence in your household or maybe this was how it was in your childhood, and that is fantastic. For me, this was new. I had never experienced this as a child or as an adult and I noticed that my heart was changing.

With each passing day, I cared less and less about work outside of a normal eight-hour workday. I began to set boundaries with my team and prioritize the needs of my family for the first time in my life. It seemed that for every minute I invested in them, I experienced hours of heartwarming fulfillment. A part of me that I had never experienced or explored was awakened and I was addicted. As Covid dragged on, and life was returning more to a normal pace at work, I began to feel resentful when I had to leave the house and be away from my family. I would leave them for the shortest period possible and knowing that each time I left the house, this virus was threatening our health and wellbeing with each exposure, my desire to focus on my career was lessening.

I would daydream about a life where I could focus on being a mother. I was realistic in my daydreams and while I knew I would not be able to be a stay-at-home mom, I dreamed about a life where there was balance. A life where I still provided and protected my children but also got a chance to experience life with them. That desire was so strong, it was consuming my thoughts.

Chapter Nine

RECONCILIATION OF THE FATHER

L ife with my dad, as a kid, was interesting. It was full of adventure and excitement which made life amusing, but it lacked any evidence of stability. For many years, I didn't know that my dad loved me. When we would spend time together, I would have a direct and indirect sense that I was not good enough. As a child this was tough, to have a sense of the abnormality of the situation without having the knowledge or understanding of what was happening.

There were times when my dad would affectionately call me "pumpkin" but most of the time, I remember him critically referring to me as "Spazella" which he would often elaborate on that "Spazella" was a stupid princess. I was pretty, but in his eyes I was dumb. In some ways, I was lucky to have an under-active or undeveloped ability to feel and express emotion, because I don't remember this hurting my feelings. I internalized his comments as part of my identity because I did not know how to take in information, process it and determine if and how it serves me. I was a little sponge, that absorbed my environment. I

In the majority of my childhood memories with my dad, they included drugs, chaos or criticism. If he planned a trip, it would end in bad situations, such as the time, we broke down in Pismo Beach, California on our way to see our family in Southern, California and we had to sleep in the bed of our pickup truck for a week or so, while he figured out a way to pay for the necessary repairs. There was very little money for food, a hotel was out of the question and the vacation was now an alternate opportunity to survive in a new and unfamiliar way. There were many times that my dad would take me out "wheeling" with him which was taking his truck off-road and attempting situations that his vehicle and I may or may not be capable of, like the time we attempted to ford a large, fast flowing river in our Toyota and were swept downstream which water poured in the windows. Since we didn't drown, he would consider that bonding. My dad's life revolved around three primary loves, vehicles, baseball and drugs. He would drag me to car shows where we would walk around for hours while he would share intricate details on hundreds of cars an hour. Looking back, I am amazed at how knowledgeable he was about cars.

We would play wiffle ball for hours in the front yard of my grandparents' house, most of the time my dad was focused on winning and not on quality time or teaching me anything about the sport, but I was a sponge and I absorbed his knowledge. My dad was very vocal when I was younger that he was disappointed that I was not a son. My gender seemed to make it difficult for him to take me seriously or have a desire to spend quality time with me. When my younger brother was born, my dad was in a blissful state. I remember thinking that life would be so much easier as a boy. Being a girl seemed to have given me a real disadvantage in life. I was easily abused, I was dumb, I was undervalued, I was second class, and I was weak. These are the things that my world was teaching me.

My dad, while he was not a traditional parent, would say to me that I could be anything that I set my mind to. I believed him, just as easily as I believed the river of insults and admonishments. This would turn out to be to my advantage, my dad taught me that I was weak and stupid but in that, I was still capable of overcoming. This would be key later in life. My dad also had two pet peeves that would shape my future as well. My dad would never be late, if he committed to being somewhere at a certain time, we would be early and never miss a time commitment. I am never late; I actually get massive anxiety when I think that I will be late to anything. Just thinking about being late, writing this, puts my stomach in knots and sets off my fight or flight response. My dad would also NEVER allow me to say "I can't"; if I were to say that I was unable to do something, he would become irate. My dad was a happy-go-lucky, laid back, charismatic stoner most of the time, unless he heard me say "I can't". That simple phase would trigger his temper in a flash.

One time, when I was about seven, we were taking our annual road trip to California, just he and I, in his tricked out, two-door, baby bear brown, Datsun 410, a prized possession. He reaches in the glovebox and pulls out a classic, crumpled up, blue bandanna and drops it in my lap and tells me to fold it for him. Well, I was staring at this bandanna for a few seconds trying to understand what he meant by folding it for him, I knew better than to ask any questions even hinting that I couldn't do it or didn't understand. I must have paused for a few seconds too long which inflamed my dad. He began screaming at me, his face was a mash-up of red stubble, pale skin and piercing blue eyes, telling me how stupid I was, how easy the task was and how disappointed and sickened he was by my inability to perform a simple task. He was so upset that took the next exit at about 80 miles an hour. Tears were streaming down my face and I was scared. My dad's face was twisted and beet red and I could barely understand what he was saying. He dramatically pulls over and tells me to get out, get out of the car right now, so I did, about 9 hours from our home, in the desert near Kings City, California, on the side of a freeway exit, I got out of the car and he drove off. One of the last things he said to me was that if I could not do something as simple as fold a bandana, then I didn't deserve to ride in his car. I stood there stunned as he drove off, not scared, but more reflective. What was wrong with me, why wasn't I able to do simple things? I wasn't upset at my dad; I was disappointed in myself. About 30 minutes later, my dad pulls back up and tells me to get back in the car, and that because I am stupid and cannot behave, we would not be going on vacation to Disneyland as planned but he would drive me back home. We drove in silence for the nine-hours back home.

There was a long gap in time after that trip before we would spend much time together, and for the next eleven years, that day would keep up separated from each other. I felt unworthy of his love, I felt stupid, and I was also afraid of how my shortcomings would make him behave so I stopped seeking out opportunities to spend time with him. In that moment, sitting alone on the side of the road, I told myself that I need to learn to be smarter so that I wouldn't end up in these situations. In my little mind, I was the problem.

I would spend the next eleven years making rebellious, dumb, risky and questionable decisions which would validate within me much of the self-doubt and judgement that I learned from how my dad treated me. My dad was nearly a non-existent person in my life during this time. He was busy with his second marriage, he children and later my youngest sister. He would also spend this time taking care of my Noni and Papa who were struggling with physical ailments, dementia and other issues related to their advanced age.

When I matured some and got through my rebellious phase and really focused on school and working as I neared the age of eighteen, I went through this freak-out period the summer before I turned seventeen. The thought came into my head that when I turned eighteen, I would lose the ability to have a relationship with my parents. At this point, I was a mother of a toddler, I had been emancipated for years, living in my own apartment and I was about to go through a regression that I would not understand. I was so distraught over not having a childhood and not being loved by my parents and feeling that the sands in the hourglass were about to run out, I sank into a deep depression and reverted back to my rebellious attitude and actions. Luckily, that phase was short lived as it didn't feel like me. I was so confused, I was not this rebellious hooligan, but I was not the adult that society expected me to be; I was a mess. It was at this time that I saw that counselor that was full of direct truths that I hated but needed, and through her guidance, I decided to attend law school. There was a private law school in my City which would allow you to be admitted without having completed a four-year degree if you tested with a high enough IQ. Well, according to my dad, I had been carrying around the title of "stupidest child" but in school, my teachers and counselors always praised me for being really smart, so I decided that I was "book smart" but fundamentally dumb and I took the test. After the test, I moved on with my life not believing that I would pass the test, and since I wouldn't have the results for a few weeks, which in my life felt like a lifetime of waiting, I began to make a different plan. When the school called a month later to tell me that I not only passed the test but that I had an "usually high IQ"; I was stunned. The first person that I wanted to call was my dad. I excitedly dialed his number and when he answered, I blurted out "Spazella, has a genius level IQ!!!, can you believe that?!?". My dad's deflated response was something to the effect of "that's great; now what are you going to do". To that question, I had no clue, I was still lost.

I desperately wanted my dad to see what others saw in me. I wanted him to be proud of me. I decided to go to school, even though I was concerned that I was not going to be smart enough, but I wanted to prove to my dad that the test wasn't wrong, he was. For two years, I would make an effort to spend time with my dad. I would invite him to my apartment to eat foods that we both loved from our joint childhood with Noni and Papa, and we would go to the movies. We found that both of us loved watching movies. Since I was an adult not dependent on him and the interactions were brief, we didn't have any conflict and we grew very close. We were becoming good friends. When I learned that I would be moving out of state with my new husband due to his military career, my dad was genuinely devastated. It felt good to finally be loved by him. Maybe not in the traditional sense, but I knew that it was the best he could offer me and it was enough for me.

The distance of living across the country would take a toll on mine and my dad's relationship and we would not see each other in person for another decade. My dad continued to live a chaotic life, although he was sober for a lot of those years, he would continue to struggle with stability. He did discover that he not only had a passion for fishing, but he was a talented fishing guide. Which is so ironic, given he is allergic to fish! He would move to Southern Oregon and spend years perfecting his skillset and growing his fishing guide business. We would speak occasionally over the years and if he ever got into a financial bind, I would help him out as best as I could. He didn't have much interest in keeping in touch, or at least it didn't feel like the connection that we built was worth maintaining. I now know that his childhood trauma and my childhood trauma left us both with extreme difficulty in creating and maintaining relationships. The silence wasn't personal on either end, we were both just living our individual lives.

Shortly after relocating back to the West Coast after being away for years, I drove to Oregon to see my dad. He was living in a trailer park on the water, in a tiny trailer without a restroom. At that moment, I realized how resilient my father was. He was living his dream as a fishing guide, living a simple life, in the best way that he knew how. He met my two other children for the first time and my new husband over a nice dinner at the restaurant there at the trailer park. I was able to meet some of my dad's friends, and it was clear that my dad was still the charismatic character that everyone loved. While the visit was nice, and it sparked the connection back, we would not stay in close contact.

A few years later, I would learn that my dad was having some health challenges which would require him to move to Southern California with an uncle of mine. My dad needed two new knees and was having some issues with his heart. My uncle was having his own physical and financial concerns and was struggling to house and care for my dad. In hearing the news, I immediately wanted him to come and live with my family and I in Washington state. I spoke to my husband and he agreed that my dad could come to stay with us temporarily.

Within a month, he was on a train with two duffle bags of stuff headed to live with me. This would be the first time we had lived together for any length of time since I was eight years old. He would live with us for the next five or so years. It was a huge adjustment for all of us. I was raising my children to be very sheltered, and I hid my past from them and those around me. My dad is very colorful and loves to share wild stories about his life. He is unconventional both as a father and as a grandpa, but there was something healing about this time we shared under one roof. My dad took an active role in helping with the kids and while he would balk at some of my parenting tactics and my food choices, he would throw a fit about having to eat quinoa, "what are we having to eat, "QUINOA?" would frequently be heard in a mocking tone"; he learned what it was like to be part of a "normal" family. My life, and the life of my children was anything but chaotic. It was very vanilla in comparison to the way he was raised and my childhood. While we both cherished and at times endured this time together, I think it was the healing that we both needed. I was able to show my dad who I was, under the "Spazella" and "worthless" labels he unfairly gave me, and I was able to learn more about what grew him into the man I experienced as a kid. Today, I know that my dad is insanely proud of me, he brags about me and my family to everyone who will listen and that was validation that I needed in order to heal. Had I not received that, I would have still healed, I know that, but the journey would have looked so differently.

Living a life based on faith, I learned that I have a redeemed relationship with Christ and that was the healthy relationship with a father that truly feeds my soul, but reconciliation with my earthly dad brought peace to my heart and healing to that wounded little girl who will forever live inside me. My healing journey needed to include the redemption God offered and the reconciliation with my dad.

Chapter Ten

ONE BOLD ASS MOVE

My newfound knowledge of that other dimension of motherhood I discovered near the start of Covid, would change my life for the better. The more I connected with this need to spend time with my husband and children, the more I could feel my heart healing. I always knew that my troubled childhood and young adult years impacted me, but since I had grown into a productive and successful member of society, I considered myself as healed.

What I wasn't aware of or what I was unwilling to acknowledge within myself is that I was not healed. The part of me that was truly broken was just as broken as could be, and by slowing down and loving my family and receiving and experiencing their love in return, I was actually healing from deep within and not the surface healing that I previously settled for. This was amazing and life changing. Here I was experiencing the most incredible growth and I realized that I could not express it to those around me. It wasn't like I was alone, I was typically surrounded by people both in person and virtually.

The issue was, very few of those people in my life knew me or anything about me below the surface. I had structured my life in a way where I was very professional both professionally and personally. I was a good listener and most of the time this meant people expected very little of me when it came to revealing things about myself. The majority of my conversations were about work, even my husband worked with me, so most of the people in my life knew him well and wouldn't think to ask any questions about our life. So here I was at a major crossroads in my life and I could only look within and look above for perspective and guidance. I prayed a lot. I would pray for direction, receive what I felt was direction and then I would pray for confirmation. What I was contemplating was going to not only change my life, but it would impact hundreds of others, some more deeply than others.

What I was feeling compelled and led to do was going to seem crazy to all my outsiders. I knew in my heart, I needed to move. The quit my job and walk away from my current life kind of move. Since I was married, the first person that I needed to share my thoughts with were my husband and the thought would literally make me nauseous. He seemed so comfortable in our lifestyle that I didn't think he would support a change. For weeks, I prayed for the courage to have that conversation, the words to start the conversation and the obedience to follow through even when it terrified me.

One day it was just Zack and I and we were commuting home together. We had nearly two hours of commuting in front of us, uninterrupted chatting time. When there was a break in the conversation, I drew in a deep breath and without taking the time to think or fear, I quickly blurted out, "what do you think about moving?". Zack responded with his desires in a new home, more land, a larger shop, areas for this and areas for that. He went on to name some suburbs that would be a closer commute to work given that our average commute was about 90 minutes each way. I think I must have given some cursory responses, "yeah babe, that sounds nice, that would be cool", etc. He was suggesting the opposite of what I was thinking. He was wanting to move to an even more expensive area to a larger and more expensive piece of property. I didn't have the ability at the time to share what I felt was a better plan. The conversation continued about what we should do to make the house sellable and how we could focus on this and that. I didn't abandon my heart's desire or what I felt I was being called to do, but I let the idea just simmer. Before I knew it, a few days later Zack had called our realtor and asked her to give us an estimate on what our home would sell for and what projects would increase the value. That next weekend, she and he were walking the property and making plans. I was both happy and sad, I knew selling the house and moving was the right thing to do, but in Zack's plan, it would mean I would need to focus even more on my career.

A few weeks and two or three home improvement projects later, I would be given another gift that would lead me in the right direction. I use the term gift because in hindsight, that is what it was but at the time it felt like a knife to the heart. My boss, the owner of the company, sent me a horrible email. The premises of the email were that I was not doing a good enough job and he was hearing complaints about my leadership, to include that all I do is hire my friends and not give everyone a fair chance. At the time, I was devastated by this email. I had dedicated nearly a decade to this company and felt that I was a caring and fair leader. I had never hired someone or promoted someone on anything but merit. I immediately responded to the email asking for direction, understanding and mentorship. If I had mis-stepped, I wanted to make things right even if I didn't agree with the harsh approach or the false accusations. I waited and waited, and no response came. Weeks went by and still no response. Interactions with him swayed between normal and passive aggressive and at times aggressive and hostile.

In this state of extreme emotional distress, I went to my husband and told him that we needed to pull our house off the market and that work was too volatile and unpredictable at this time. I was a mess, I put so much stock into my career that this behavior and lack of response was truly painful. I was experiencing stress like never before, to the point I was physically ill and not sleeping. The relationships all around me were suffering and I felt so alone and confused. What I couldn't see in that moment was God preparing my heart for what needed to happen next. Now, I had the courage to share with Zack what I had originally planned to share, I felt that God was calling us to a simpler life far from our current life. When I told him what had been on my heart, I was genuinely amazed at his response. He was fully onboard with exploring my idea. Now, this was extremely out of character for him. He was very happy with his job, our lifestyle, he had never really lived outside of the Seattle area, his friends, family, hobbies and interests were all focused here. He immediately said, let's explore this idea more. I shared with him that I felt that I was supposed to move to Kentucky. This was so far-fetched to him given we had no real knowledge of Kentucky. He jumped right in and started researching different states and the pros and cons of each area. He wanted trees and greenery and a landscape that would allow him to pursue his passion for the outdoors. I didn't stop him looking into other areas even though I felt strongly where we were moving to, if we could move.

A few weeks and lots of researching and conversations later, Zack was skeptical but willing to travel with me to Kentucky to explore the possibility. We had a trip to Mexico planned and instead of flying to Mexico we exchanged our tickets for tickets to Nashville, Tennessee which was the closest airport the airline flew into. Zack had taken the lead on planning the trip, securing a realtor, planning and everything that went with this crazy idea. Days before we flew out, we called our real estate agent and asked her to put our house on the market, that our plan to move was back on. She confirmed that the house would be live the day we landed in Tennessee.

We only had a long weekend to look at homes, so our schedule was jam packed. I think we looked at fifty homes that weekend. Our real estate agent in Kentucky was a little mesmerized by our craziness, but he was a good sport and was more than willing to not only show us homes all over the area, but also try and orientate us to the cultural, geographical and other differences that we may need to know in order to make an informed decision on moving. Day one of the house hunting experience was a bust. The homes we were seeing in person were unlike the homes we had viewed online. After a ten- hour day or house hunting we were both feeling defeated and in part I think we both thought the other one was a little silly for their willingness to go along with this hairbrained scheme. Day two started out much of the same. We saw a few homes that were OK, but none that we were in love with. We realized pretty quickly that downsizing our lives and lifestyle was more than shallow thoughts, we would need to adjust our expectations. Sure, we could afford a nicer, larger and perceived "better" home than the price range we were looking at, but it would defeat the purpose of moving and downsizing our lives and expenses. We knew that if we stuck to the financial part of the plan, we would be able to walk away from our home in Washington completely debt free, with money to put down on a reasonably priced home in Kentucky and still have money to put into savings. We could not let our egos, or our tainted desires deter us from our solid plan. I think halfway through day two of the hunt, we emotionally gave up and thought "well if nothing else this was an adventure". I went to bed the night of day two feeling defeated and I silently asked God what happened. The vision was so clear, and I have been so obedient so why was the trip turning out so shitty and unfruitful? I fell asleep without clarity.

We woke up the next morning with only a few hours of house hunting scheduled before we needed to head back to the airport in Tennessee. Zack had expended his frustrations the night before by aggressively looking online at homes, and bombarding our nice agent with potential options for our final day of searching. The agent was only able to confirm three showings for that third day. The first one we were meeting at, he had not planned to show us but added it at the last minute and two more that he wasn't sure we would actually like after getting to know us that weekend but he would show them. We set out that morning apprehensive that the day would be a bust.

The first home was about thirty minutes outside of the City. I was concerned with commute times after spending years in arduous commutes and wasted hours of my life, but I had agreed that thirty minutes was my max commuting willing-ness. We were running a little early, so we drove through town, a town that was so picturesque I nearly asked Zack to pinch me. The streets were full of historic buildings, lined with cute shops, restaurants, coffee shops and galleries. There was a large town square and a farmers' market. The home we were to look at was just a few streets over from this area. As we pulled into the driveway of the most quaint and storybook looking, brick home, I said to Zack before the car was even in park, that this was my home. He looked at me and said, "chill out, we haven't even seen inside of it yet". I just knew, my heart knew. I felt more drawn to this home than any home we had looked at that day and any home I had lived into date. The connection for me was more than how it looked, or the location, both of which were great, it stirred something deep in me. That feeling was in line with these new feelings I had with motherhood and family life.

I needed this home.

Now, for Zack, this home was the opposite of what he was looking for. It was in a town when he dreamed of remote acreage. It was a multi-story brick home with a small, detached garage, no shop in sight and being in the historical district, there was no ability to add a shop later. It was on a busy road, which he said he would never live on because there was no sense of privacy and he is a very private person. For everything that was "right" for me, it was "wrong" for him. I knew what that meant, you see in our marriage most things went his way as I would pick my battles carefully. As much as I wanted this house, I was unwilling to fight about it. I put on my best "happy wife mask" and we continued to look at the other homes on the list.

The next two homes were not far away, and the showings went by quickly and without much affection. They were again OK homes but not what we wanted. Zack surprised me by asking if we could go back and look at that first home again. Not wanting to jinx it, I played it very cool even though I was giddy inside. I wanted to ask him what he was thinking and if we might buy that house, but inside I rode in silence. When we pulled back into the driveway, I couldn't help but to smile. A smile so big, I could not hide it. We walked through the house, entering each room with careful inspection. It seemed that Zack was strongly considering the home. We were there long enough to where the agent said he had to lock up and go, and we knew that we had better get going too.

Zack wanted to drive down the alley behind the house to see what it looked like from that angle before we left. As we pulled into the alley, there was an older man in the alley taking out his trash. Zack, who is not a small talker, rolled down his window and started talking to this man. I was shocked, who was this man that looked like my husband. This man who was laughing and joking with this stranger? I was liking this version of him. It turns out that the man who was taking out his trash, was the Mayor of the town and a lifelong town resident. He gave us such great history on the house and the area along with a really welcomed feel.

We drove away both feeling so happy and connected to a place that we had not heard of until this day. As we drove out of town, just before you entered the on ramp to the interstate, there was a large sign that read "Welcome to the Kindness Capitol of Kentucky". I thought to myself, thank you God for yet another sign.

During the three-hour drive back to the airport, we had a lot to discuss. Were we moving, did we find a house, what were the next steps, were we nuts? All these things and more were discussed.

We decided that as crazy as it sounded, as bizarre as the whole thing was, Kentucky was where we both wanted to be. While the weekend was not ideal, there was a lack of clarity of what the future would bring, we both felt connected to the area. This was refreshing, exciting, and terrifying all at once. We called the realtor and made an offer on the home that I loved in the "Kindness Capital of Kentucky".

While all this house hunting was occurring in Kentucky, our home was being shown back in Washington. Within a day of showings, we had multiple offers over asking price which we happily accepted. While we knew we would not be moving right away, we were willing to move quickly to sell our home which would close within 30 days and live temporarily in an Airbnb while we looked for jobs and waited to close on our new home in Kentucky.

That plan sounded great, but it wouldn't be my life if it worked out that smoothly. We learned the next day that our offer was not accepted. The buyer went with another offer which was higher than ours. We stuck to our plan and refused to offer more as this house was at the top of our planned budget already. I was sad, I had really thought this was to be our house.

We got back online and started looking at more homes in Kentucky, armed with our new knowledge of what areas we liked and disliked. We found a few homes we could live with but not make a life in. We both knew that these new options were not the one. We tried not to feel discouraged or argue and fight from the stress, which was hard. We were under such a large amount of stress and from all areas of our life. We had not wanted to complicate our life further by sharing that we planned to move, especially since the move was still months away and we needed to find a house and jobs. We just didn't have answers for ourselves let alone the world who wouldn't understand.

A week or so after we returned home to Washington, we heard from our agent that the home we had made an offer on was back on the market after their contract fell through. We immediately made an offer and they accepted it. I was overjoyed. I felt that it was in essence a reward for our patience and willingness to continue to move forward even when we didn't know what was ahead.

I began my job hunt and within weeks had interviewed and was offered a position in Louisville. I felt like life was falling into place. There was still so much to prepare for and so many unknowns but overall our plan was taking shape.

Feeling that the plan was taking shape in no way meant that it was easy or that I was fully confident in my decision.

While I was remarkably surprised that there had been such co-operation from Zack and a lack of strong opposition from the kids, I still felt the weight of the world on my shoulders. It was not the move itself that was stressing me, as I felt so strongly that God was calling us to Kentucky; my concerns were with myself. There has been a deep-seated feeling within the recessed parts of me, that feels that I will not experience a peaceful life. I am rarely ever content, comfortable or at peace. I appear to be duck, gliding gracefully on the top of the water, but just beneath the surface if anyone were close enough to see, they would see that I am kicking my legs hard and rapidly just to appear picturesque on the surface. I was recently asked if I considered myself a routine person or a risk taker and as much as I wanted to be able to say routine, that would be a lie. There is nothing routine about my life. My best laid plans are usually very flexible. While I will not allow myself to miss a commitment, a deadline or be late to something, I live my life is a fluid manner. When I think about why that is, I see that the pattern is I am dependable, structured, and reliable when there is someone else relying on me. If the only person I must let down or be responsible for is myself, I am not as disciplined. I dislike that about myself. I have come to terms with this being my baseline character, but I am constantly challenging myself to be there for myself and treat myself as I treat others. One of my failings as a parent for years was that I treated my children as an extension of myself instead of an independent person. When I realized that they were independent of me with their own needs, personalities, and dreams I became a better parent. I switched from a self-sacrificing mindset to a giving and providing mindset.

The move to Kentucky is incredibly symbolic in hindsight. Our family has never been happier or healthier. We have been able to create the life that we wanted here. We are truly engineering every part of our life with intent and purpose. From the way that we are designing our backyard to be a place for community gathering, to the business we are in the process of building in faith that it will help others on their journey, to the time we are spending as a family. We are able to take the aspects of our lives together, our lives apart and the dreams we have and are focusing on creating the life that we desire. To say we have never been happier is an understatement.

I am so blessed to already be seeing positive changes in my family from these intentional efforts. We are so connected, we spend time together, we talk, the kids are interested in being a part of the family, they have even suggested that we continue to reduce screen time to be able to spend more time together. I would have never imagined that this would be the case. My husband is enjoying making friends and having idle conversations with everyone he meets. There is a sense of peace and calm in each of us that did not exist in our previous environment. That connection that I desperately craved, now exists within my own family.

I can see now that I was so absorbed in my efforts to make a good living that I missed the point of having a good life. I know better understand the saying, "you cannot heal in the same place where you got sick". For me, this has a figurative and literal meaning and for my healing journey, I need to take action to grow in a place where I chose to be planted.

Chapter Eleven

THE STABLE LOVE OF GROWTH

While so much of my growth occurred organically stemming from natural maturing with age and a wealth of life experience; I also intentionally sought out opportunities to grow. Learning and school was what was constant in my life. It was what made me feel stable and safe.

We all grow differently, some learn best by experiencing something, some by hearing it, some by reading or seeing it. I have found that I grow best when I connect with something. When a subject or idea doesn't excite me or create a feeling of connection, I have very little motivation to pursue it. I am highly relational and learn best from and beside others. Stories deeply impact me. I am a lover of all documentaries, and it is rarely the subject matter that draws me in. It is the approach, unveiling an idea, thought, event or experience in a way where I can see and feel all the dimensions of it at once. I realized that the combination of sound and images draws me in quickly and closely. What I observed while tuning in and observing my own thoughts, reactions and behaviors is when I am told information in a straightforward way, it is blah to me. I may have some interest in the subject matter, but I will unlikely take that surface level information and retain it or learn it.

When the same information is presented to me in story format, something sticks, when I have an opportunity to relate to it or see how someone else has been impacted by it, I am intrigued and primed to learn and grow. I have learned so much by listening to people talk, sometimes it is the direct content but oftentimes it is how they perceived the experience and how they retell it. I am so engaged listening to the said and unsaid of the story, the why, the experience.

Armed with this knowledge of how I engage and learn best, it opened me up to a real ability to grow and change. I had always liked books and would be known to read for pleasure but as I aged and my life got busier, I took less and less time to read. I saw therapists on and off for years, but I hated talking about myself and would often find myself "interviewing" my therapist trying to understand them and their lives better. I got more out of their story and how they reacted to life and what drove their decisions than me telling my story and experience and hearing their well-intentioned, educated and canned responses. I found that therapists do not like to talk about themselves, they like to maintain "professional boundaries" which I respect and totally understand, but that boundary limits me and my ability to grow.

In 2013, I discovered Audible to entertain myself during long commutes. This was life changing and it allowed me to listen to stories for hours on end. I could listen to professional development books, self-help books, biographies, the options were endless. I have consistently listened to 2-3 books a week for the past seven years. That is a lot of knowledge! Now, not every book was helpful to me, or life changing, or motivating but I will say that being armed with this tool, was the start of me becoming a better person, a more successful person, a better mom, and a better leader.

I loved sharing the knowledge I was spending my time absorbing. I was recommending books to those in my life, sharing tidbits of information and through these interactions, I was developing my purpose. I enjoyed helping others grow, develop, and learn. I was coaching and mentoring those around me, and I was the healthiest mentally as I had even been. Being in my element and being healthier was a match for my growing career. I was known as a good leader, kind, emotionally intelligent and kind. It was easier to apply the things I was learning to my work environment and since I was seeing tremendous results, that is where I focused. I tried to listen to books that had more direct topics related to parenting, marriage and trauma and I struggled connecting to these books. Why!?! Why was this strategy not working in the areas that I needed the most? It came down to my brokenness. I was still wounded in these areas. I thought I was healed because other areas of my life had improved, and I had grown in so many other areas.

It is part of our human nature to treat the symptoms of something and not the root cause. This is as true of trauma as it is of physical ailments. If I have a headache, I am likely going to pop a Tylenol, down some water and hope it goes away. If I have a runny nose, I may take an allergy medicine and go on with my day. Our society has made it easy to treat symptoms and much harder to treat root causes. This is the same for trauma. I have suffered from anxiety, an inability to connect with others, depression, isolation, eating disorders, substance abuse and other self-destructive behaviors. I was self-treating the symptoms that were stemming from my trauma, neglect, and abuse.

I didn't want to behave in a self-deprecating manner. There were so many times when I was so desperate to end the cycle of chaos that I was living in that I would have given anything to feel relief. What I wanted was an easy solution. What I wanted was to not have to "deal" with my past because it would require me to reopen the wounds to heal from them. I tried everything to avoid this. I didn't have a chemical imbalance, but I took antidepressants. When they didn't cure the pain and stop the negative behaviors, I would declare to anyone who would listen, that doctors know nothing.

I wasn't an addict, but there were years when I drank and consumed substances that would numb me from having to face the demons that were dragging me down. I wanted to be fit and healthy, but I would eat sugar and fatty foods to boost my moods and provide temporary energy boosts.

I wanted a happy family, but I would say hateful things to my husband to push him away to prevent more inevitable heartache and pain. I wanted an abundant social life, but I would wear my mask, keep people at a distance, rarely reveal more about me than what was at surface level and isolate. I was structuring my life in a way that would provide me as much security as possible, but this life would not provide me happiness. I was armed with a lot of knowledge and had the tools available to change, but I was so reluctant.

I knew that real healing would hurt first, and it would cause me to have to make changes in how I was living. By the time, I was ready for this true step of deep healing, I had abandoned most of the self-destructive habits. I had done away with any bad habit that would threaten the healthy part of my life-my career. What was left for me to heal from was the tough stuff, the relationship issues, the relationship I had with my husband, kids, close friends and those in my family that I still had contact with. The reason why this group was so hard to heal with is it required ultimate vulnerability. I had to share my dark truths, my shortcomings, and my needs all at once. Those people that relied on me so heavily would see the weakness in me, and what if they abandoned me like my mother had? The fear was so real that I could feel its presence in a room with me. As I would interact with my close circle, I would be faced with this barrier again and again. When I realized that it was not a barrier at all, it was a choice, I was empowered to change.

With each interaction, I had a choice on if I was going to be vulnerable or cold. If I would share my fears or hold them in. Over time, and with a lot of practice, I began seeing that my fears were much larger in my head than they were in real life. These choices I were making were choices like instead of berating my husband for a mistake that he made, I would say quiet and not hold a grudge or act out in hostility. When he was pushing my buttons, I would respond with patience and kindness. When we would have a fight, I would plan a date night at a special restaurant rather than hold on to my frustrations for weeks and allow them to eat me up inside and grow into a silent rage.

When my children would come home from school, I would ask them about their day and not a cursory ask but shutting down my laptop, turning my phone over and giving them my undivided attention. I would look for opportunities to spend time with them and listen to them. None of these changes amounted to anything overnight. It would take consistently on my part to build their trust. When they would hurt me by not responding in the way I had hoped or not wanting to spend time with me, I would share that it hurt me, and I would not react in anger.

My growth was happening, and I was growing in my confidence. Having some success in healing my marriage and family relationships, I was slowly opening up to my friends. I was beginning to share some of the backstory that made me who I am. I would share opinions even when I knew they wouldn't be popular or well received. I would be kind and honest above all else. I was treating people the way I wanted to be treated.

Now, the story is not all butterflies and rainbows, not at all. I was so focused on my own brokenness and healing from my brokenness, that it did not occur to me that I would be wounded intentionally by people I had grown to trust. This was a great lesson and a true test of my newfound healing; I did not react in anger when I was hurt or betrayed. In fact, it had been so long since I had let anyone in that close to me, that I was almost thankful for the opportunity the hurt brought me. How would I know that I was healing, that I had grown or evolved if I were never tested?

Chapter Twelve

GROWING IN GRACE

I am a strong believer in God, but I often fail to yield to him and rely on him. Growing up the way I did, without a base of faith, love, security, or peace I only knew how to survive based on my own strength and knowledge. More recently on my faith journey, I read "Sometimes when you wonder why you can't hear God's voice during your trials. Remember the teacher is always quiet during the test". I am almost embarrassed to say this was a meme I read on Facebook and it had a profound impact on my perspective.

Since becoming a Christian, I have felt the presence of God so strongly in my life even when I wasn't living faithfully. Most of the time, I took the comfort of His presence for granted and would go about my day, sometimes remembering to pray but most of the time I was too busy. I may not have taken the time to thank and acknowledge God, but I would immediately recognize the times when I did not feel Him close to me. I mentioned earlier in the book that I rarely feel at peace or settled, this is true, but God's presence has been a comforter to me. It may not completely take away my struggles but there is a different energy about me when I don't have Him in my life. When I was going through the two years of intense personal growth. Chipping away at the deep ugly stuff that had been dragging me down for years, He was there with me. On the days I would willfully call out to him, he was there and, on the days, when I was strong enough on my own, He was there. Until He wasn't.

Even though I have been told repeatedly that there is nothing I can do to earn God's love, I was pretty convinced he was proud of my works and was secretly favoring me because of them. So, when all hell broke out in my life, when my job was destabilized, when my friends began to turn on me, when my family felt I was losing it, when I was needing that peace and grace the most, I felt God's distance from me. Immediately, I searched my soul for the record book I had been keeping of all the good works I have done. I helped this person, and that person, I was kind when I was wounded, I was generous, I was loving, I volunteered, etc. This mental record book of good deeds felt thick with all my hard work, so why was God absent? Why wasn't He protecting me? Didn't He remember how hard of a life He delivered me from? Didn't I deserve an easier life? I had become so comfortable with the idea of abandonment that

I assumed God would just as easily walk away from me when I no longer met His expectations. While this may be true of every human on this planet, I know better about God's character. In my moment of pain and weakness, I might have been distracted or blinded, but in my heart, I know He will never leave me. When I saw that meme about the teacher being quiet during the test, it clicked for me. I am still learning about healthy parent and child relationships, so I might not always recognize what my heavenly father is doing to help me grow, but I know about school and so that meme clicked. God had not abandoned me; he was seeing how much I had grown and learned and where he needed to continue to refine and shape me.

I actively pursue God now, not because I want something from him. He isn't a genie granting magical wishes, but rather he is the one relationship that I can trust is always full of goodness. He is for me and never against me. There were many years of my life where I would not boldly say these things for fear I would be abandoned by more people. There was a time not so long ago in my life where I would have omitted God from my story to not offend others, to not pressure others to believe my beliefs. I realize now that by not sharing my story, all the parts of my story, from the abuse to the salvation, I would be shorting the people who needed to hear my story in order to begin their healing journey. Telling me what to do on a plain white sheet of paper, in a book or while I was relaxing in a therapist's office would have never been enough to change me. I needed people to share their story to unlock my healing.

Chapter Thirteen

MY LEGACY AND DREAMS

A s strong as I have grown as a survivor of compound childhood trauma, that is not what I want to be known for. I want to be known and remembered for my kindness and love of people. I feel such immense joy when I am in service to others, when I can help them see a part of them that I see, help them heal and help them grow. I got a taste of the potential impact a good leader can have on a person's life when I was working as the Company President of that property management company. I was able to see what a hand up could do for a person who is homeless, a women fleeing her abuser, the talented person passed over by their current company because they weren't part of the "in" crowd, the person coming back out of retirement with a wealth of knowledge but age not on their side, the person whose career was a bust because they struggled with mental health issues that made them slightly unreliable and many others with trauma and human conditions most of us can relate to. The world can be a harsh place and kindness and faith can turn that around.

The lesson I learned was that I can lead an organization, but I cannot create an alignment of values in a company that I don't own. My goal is to build a company who honors people who are trying to overcome their challenges and make a living for themselves and their families. A place where it is ok to be different, to be a survivor, to march to a different tune, to have opposing beliefs and to be cherished for the uniqueness in each of us. I would love to see a moment in the world that focused more on appreciation of people than persecution and judgment of them. A culture that won't stop until the basic needs of each person in their community is met and abundance is a gift to be bestowed on your neighbors where they are friends or strangers. I may not live long enough to see this type of environment arise in our broken world, but for each day I live on this Earth, I will strive to live this way and look for those who want the same. For me, life is meant to be grown through and not just survived. With each day we are given, we have a choice on how we can choose to live and behave. Choose kindness, choose love, choose healing, choose generosity and see how your life and community evolves.

EPILOGUE

There may be people who read this, who were or are part of my story, it is my hope for you that this is your aha moment of understanding. Whatever you thought about me, however you labeled or loved me, this is my why. This is the journey of how I became me. This is my why.

For those of you who are reading this, and you are not part of my story, this book is written for you. Your story is important, and it has a purpose. Whether you have lived a life that is so good from the start that it is fairytale-like, or you endured pain and trauma that mirrors or overshadows my story, there is someone out there needing to hear your story to heal or grow. I wholeheartedly believe that we were wired for community and connection and by actively pursuing both we will be fulfilling some of our most primal emotional needs. You may be a person who has great faith or perhaps you have yet to explore that aspect of your life. Wherever you are in your faith journey, I want to share with you what I had wished I had been told as a child, God loves you, he treasures you and if given the opportunity He wants to grow in relationship with you. Had I known this sooner, it would not have saved me from my pain and trauma, but it would have helped me feel comforted and connected when the world around me was hurting me, judging me and abandoning me.

Trauma can be survived, and a beautiful life can be built from a painful foundation. The power is within us. It lies in our everyday choices and decisions. We can decide if we will heal or hurt. Once we know this about ourselves, we are empowered to build the life we want on the foundation we choose. Be strong in your journey, ask for help when you need it and know that you are loved.

ABOUT THE AUTHOR

Ella Frick

Ella Frick is the author behind the memior Growing Through It: Surviving Childhood Trauma, Abuse and Neglect. She hosts the healing podcast by the same name. She is a national speaker, certified life coach, mentor, documentarian, photographer, and suvivor advocate. Her work across multiple disciplines broadly addresses narratives of human experience. She lives a peace centered life in the "Kindess Capital of Kentucky" with her husband, and her two youngest children.

Made in the USA
Monee, IL
17 April 2021